SPIRITUAL LAW

IN THE

NATURAL WORLD,

———————

BY
EMMA CURTIS HOPKINS
&
ELEVE

———————

*Author of "Life is Worth Living," "Drops*
*of Gold," "Progress of the Pilgrim," etc.,*

———————

THIRD THOUSAND

———————

1894:
Purdy Publishing Co., Publishers
McVickers Building
Chicago

Printed by the Purdy Publishing Company

# PREFACE.

———

Readers, I expect this book to do for you what it has done for myself. I may expect even more for the principles herein set forth are ever increasing in their miracle working efficiency.

H. M. Stowe

# Introduction
## By Rev. Natalie R. Jean

Spiritual Law in The Natural World is a fabulous book written by Emma Curtis Hopkins and Eleve (H.M. Stowe). Eleve was a student of Emma Curtis Hopkins. Eleve in French means "Student." It is believed that "Eleve" put some of Emma's lessons together to form this wonderful book. It is an extremely rare book. This was a labor of love. I retyped the whole book myself, adding notes pages and a wonderful picture of Emma. Spiritual Law in The Natural World reminds me of Scientific Christian Mental Practice. Just like Scientific, it is a great book of study. As you begin to read this book, you will see the similarities between the two books. This book reawakens the Truth about our connection to source in how it relates to the spiritual world. Each passage in this book will give you the AHA!! moment that you are seeking. You will never hunger to understand your connection to God, for Emma brings you to your Freedom. Emma Curtis Hopkins was truly a wonderful Spirit. Her destiny was to bring the Truth to the world. I am blessed to be able to bring these teachings to you. I believe that it is great gift to understand what love truly means. Emma shows us how to love ourselves, to never doubt or fear, but to embrace our perfection.

# INTRODUCTION
## BY
### EMMA CURTIS HOPKINS

When we read the written thoughts of an author we are able to tell by the feelings that stir us, irrespective of our convictions, as to what the independent power of the author must be. There are certain writings which convince us almost against our will that their premises and reasoning are right, yet we feel no uplifting, no healing of bodily or mental conditions from reading them. This indicates that the hearts of the writers did not burn within them while they wrote. SPIRITUAL LAW IN THE NATURAL WORLD was the outspeaking of a hear that burned within the author, as the hearts of the two traveling from Emmaus ages ago, because her life had been spared, her strength renewed, her health restored, her hope revived by the teaching she records.

Therefore we hear from every quarter of all this same ministry which this book has already wrought for many others also. Lionel Beale told Joseph Cook that what is now wanted is something to upset natural law. By "natural law" he meant the procession of undesirable phenomena to which our race seems subjected. What shall upset diseases, starvation, hatred, pain, death, save the spirit of the "Law of the Spirit of Life in Christ Jesus, that maketh free from the law of sin and death?" He spoke what our world has long felt, viz., that we hunger and thirst for peace and safety, for health and sweet life, and realize that the methods so long in practice have signally failed to bring them. I can set to my seal that "SPIRITUAL LAW IN THE NATURAL WORLD" contains the stepping stones to every attainment the heart aspires to. It is sure to heal you if you read it-heal you of pain, of physical disease, of feebleness, of indeterminate will, of faltering by the wayside of your human walk. It will uplift, and cheer and inspire you, and this is the mission of a good book.

# CONTENTS

# CHAPTER I.

## Universal Presence of A Creator – Life Principle.

Scientific doctrine can only be established by scientific reasoning, as science means philosophical knowledge or the knowledge of reasoning.

To convince you of the reasonableness of anything we must begin our argument at some point where we agree and reason from that to establish our own ground as right.

This is the way we proceed in teaching the science of Spiritual Law, which is in itself pure reasoning, and when understood, will change the life of the world, giving joy for sadness, health for sickness, peace for discord and truth where error has reigned.

Are we not all and every one seeking to be entirely satisfied with life? We go to and fro, wander here and there-ever-restless-trying to find what will completely fill our lives, heart and minds, so that there will be nothing left to desire.

Has anybody ever found this entire content-or satisfaction-in the prevailing theologies, philosophies, sciences, or transcendentalisms of the past? All have striven, labored, studied to reach this goal, but not one ever attained it in its full completeness except Jesus Christ.

If He attained satisfaction why has not his example been followed? Why have we not been understood, and his life has seemed too hard to imitate in this prosaic, materialistic world.

Not only that, but all who have considered him to be God have been too busy discussing speculative theories concerning him to literally follow him. But there is no other way. "I am the truth," *** "follow me," he said.

We have never found the truth in his teaching, for it has been covered with rubbish of ceremonial, with dogma and creed for generation after generation, till, like the strata of geology, there has formed layer upon layer of crustacean covering, and become like the kernel of a nut within its shell so hard that it requires an effort to break and throw off before the hidden meat is exposed to view.

The science of Spiritual Law removes the shell of speculations and gives us the truth as Jesus gave it, unvarnished, unadorned and in its purity. There is, therefore, nothing new in it, and those who expect something totally unknown heretofore are often disappointed in its first lessons, and sometimes a feeling of irritation arises and young students think this science cannot be so wonderful or bring such great power if it is the same old story. But truth misunderstood is not truth to that one who misunderstands it. Truth perverted is not truth at all. Truth unused is not existent to that one who neglects it.

If people had spoken Truth one millionth part as much as they have talked of all other things, it would have prevailed by this time to our satisfaction. It is truth understood, truth used, truth lived, that will bring heaven into view, or, as we are in the habit of expressing it, bring a new heaven and a new earth.

It does make all things new. Let us try to grasp it, to get such a hold upon it that we become one with it. Let us eat the words of truth and so assimilate them that they are the life current that flows through us with a richness unparalleled, giving us true health, real strength and the vitality that only God can impart.

Now in order to explain how the Truth works we *meta* go back to the early discovery of mental law and show how Mind works, for Truth can work only through Mind. Thus we must first of all understand Mind.

The study of Mind is the study of metaphysics, for meta means above-out of range of-so metaphysics is out of the range of physics, which is the study of knowledge of the material world, then it must be of mind, as all that is above what we call materiality is certainly mind.

All philosophers have taught that there is a first cause of all things, whether they call it Nous or Air or Substance, and that this Cause is Divine. Metaphysicians have gone farther and said that mind was the cause of all things, though some of them have called mind a human product of materiality.

All who have made a study of the Cause of all things have become so at one with it as to have causing power, for it is an invariable rule that we become like what we study or are closely associated with. We become so like people with whom we live constantly that often the expression of face and sound of voice grow similar, and even the features grow alike. Sometimes a child will look more like its nurse than its mother.

Those ancient students of power found themselves invested with power even over material things, for they caused corn to grow, roses to bloom, rain to fall or cease, empty cruses to be filled with oil and measures of meal to increase by word or will. By words the sick were healed and the dead raised, and the words so used were called Truth.

Those students of First Cause who had such power through their study called the Cause God, and down to this day It is called God. The words that had such healing potency were called the word of God or Truth.

Truth was called the Substance of all, the Origin of all and the Ruler of all, and pure Intelligence. Then those words were words of Substance, Life and Intelligence, and as they were words of God, God must be Substance, Life and Intelligence.

We should never condemn a person unheard. It is not only unjust but not according to law and equity. Neither should we condemn a subject or doctrine unheard and unknown. To do so is evidence of a small, narrow, prejudiced mind.

Spiritual Law is the teaching of Jesus Christ. How can any one dare to condemn knowledge of Christ's teaching either heard or unheard. Jesus said that certain signs should follow those who believed in him and his doctrine, and those signs now follow all who truly accept His doctrine of Spiritual Law.

The study of mind or metaphysics, or more strictly speaking the science of mind, has three departments-Therapeutic, or the healing of the body by means of the mind, through the influence of right thoughts. Ethical, showing how thought forms the character. It also teaches the laws and conditions of right thinking.

Religious-treating of Mind, Soul and Spirit, showing them to be identical in essence. It proves each mind or soul to be made by and in the image of the Divine Soul or Mind, and to be one with that Universal Mind. Never to have "fallen" from that oneness for the thought and the mind that thinketh are one and the same and we are the thoughts of the Mind that is God.

The problem that the race has ever tried and is still trying to solve, is how to get satisfaction. It is the problem of life. Is there a solution of it?

When we would solve a problem in mathematics we study the principle of mathematics involved, and its rules. Then if we would solve the problem of life we must find out and study the Principle of Life.

Now this Principle must be the Cause of all life, and the cause or beginning of life has been called creation. Then it is the truth concerning creation that we want in order to know from whence we came and why. The only one who ever reached the solution of this problem, said, "Search the Scriptures," and in them we find an account of creation saying, "In the beginning God created."

Then God is the Principle of Life: He is the Principle we are to study, and in order to do so we must know the truth about Him. Like Pilate, we ask, "What is the truth?"

Jesus said, "I Am the Truth," "I and my Father are one;" and "I ascend to my Father and to your Father and to my God and your God."

Then he was one with God, and if Jesus was Truth God must be Truth. When we find Truth we find the Life Principle and find that it is God.

God in all languages is called Good, so it is the Good that is the Principle of Life-that is Truth. Jesus said God is Spirit, then Spirit is the Principle of Life. He also said God is Love, then Love is the Principle of Life.

If God creates He must sustain, uphold and support his creations. Then He must be unchangeable, steadfast, immutable and eternal, or Substance. Then Substance is the Life Principle.

Philosophers have said that First Cause was Substance. Whether philosophers have named the First Cause God or not, they have said it was Intelligence. Intelligence is surely Mind and God is Mind, then God is Intelligence and Intelligence is the Life Principle.

We have found what God, or the Principle of Life is, now we must know where it is.

It is not said of any but God that He created. Then God created all that is, and wherever He created there He must be, so He is Omnipresent, for the work of creating never ceases as it never began.

"The real meaning of, "In the beginning God created' is, In the Great Forever without beginning of years or end of days God is creating or creates." The Good then is everywhere in all places. Life is good, then Life is everywhere, for there is no place where Life is not Good and Good is everywhere.

Because people get tired of living in the material world is no proof that real life is not good, for such have not found true life at all. They are selfish and think only of the gratification of their human desires. That is not life.

Love is Good, then as Good is everywhere Love must be everywhere.

God is Truth and God is everywhere present, then Truth is everywhere and all there is for Truth is Good.

Substance is everywhere because it is Good and Good is everywhere.

Intelligence is Good and Good is in all places, thus Intelligence is all there is.

As Good is the Cause of all, there can be nothing caused or existent except Good. Good fills all space, then there can be no room for evil. There never could have been any creation except good, then evil does not, cannot, never did exist. This is truth.

The Good, or God, is Spirit, then as Good is Omnipresent, Spirit must fill all space. As Spirit fills all space there is no place for matter. This is truth.

As Love is Omnipresent there can be nothing contrary to Love. All is Love. This is truth. We do not mean the selfishness that thinks some one does not love us enough. That is mortal or human love which is not true love at all.

Paul described real Love. It is divine and is God.

Truth is God and God is Omnipresent, then Truth is everywhere to the exclusion of error or falsehood.

Intelligence is Mind, Mind is Spirit and Spirit is Omnipresent, then there is naught but Intelligence in the universe.

Life is everywhere and good, then there is no death. Life cannot be interrupted for Life is God. This is truth.

Now we know what and where the Principle us by which we are to solve our problem of life, but before we can get the correct answer we must see if we have hithero had any errors in our work.

In mathematics all errors must be erased or the answer will be all wrong. There is a way to know whether the answer is right or wrong and that is, to prove the example. If it will not prove we look for errors till we find them and then erase such.

It our life problem is not right, if it does not prove by bringing satisfaction, we must look for the errors in our statements concerning the principle.

If we believe that there is another power beside The Good we have an error to erase. If we believe in any other substance than Spirit we have an error to erase. If we believe that anything except Love fulfills the Law we have an error to erase. If we believe in any possibility other than Life Eternal we have an error to erase.

If we do not correctly state our propositions we must not expect our problem to be correct in its solution.

What are the results that prove that our problem is correctly solved?

The sick and helpless are well and strong. The sad and sorrowful are joyous and glad. The cross and evil-tempered are kind and pleasant. The poor have plenty. The vicious are reformed; bad habits and appetites drop away as the dead leaves from a tree. The cold and skeptical become devout and believing. These changes do not come about through pleading, begging, haranguing, or by manipulation, herbs and drugs, or drinks and appliances. Health comes by the power of the silent word, or the word of Truth spoken in the silence. Happiness and peace come by the use of the silent word. A new sweet character comes by the power of the silent word.

There is nothing that cannot be done through the silent word of Truth as thousands are testifying continually.

By knowing the Life Principle and the laws of mind concerning right thinking any one can bring the beautiful result of the perfect satisfaction to his problem of life.

The mind must be cleansed of all prejudice, all uncharitableness, all narrowness.

Right thinking understood teaches only the best, highest and purest thoughts and will bring peace and happiness, and heal and spiritualize the whole character which will show forth in a perfect body.

We can cure disease in others by thoughts and prevent disease in self or others by thoughts.

We then know how to keep from wrong judgments; how to be wise and strong of mind; how to be hopeful and joyous by making our surroundings hopeful and joyous.

No one can be foolish, ignorant or unhappy who understands the science of Mind and Spirit.

The proving of our problem is proving ourselves good and spiritual instead of sinful and material; peaceful in mind and sound of body; so filled with Truth that all clouds of earthly experience are dispersed, showing a rainbow of hope, faith and understanding, with the full assurance there is but one God, whose name is Good and that to us belong all His benefits.

# NOTES

# NOTES

CHAPTER II.

**Rejection of Error.**

The scientific doctrine of Spiritual Law is Truth, and Truth can only be comprehended by mind. Then we must understand mind in order to get hold of Truth in the right way and in a firm and unwavering manner.

To understand mind and all its operations, in a scientific manner, we must study it.

Now, scientific knowledge is systematic knowledge; so to understand mind in a scientific way, is to have a systematic knowledge of mind and its ways, so our study must have a system-one step at a time.

We learned in the first lesson, or statement of Being, that the only Real Being that exists, or the Creative Energy called by all God, is Spirit, Intelligence, Divine Mind, and is everywhere present, all powerful and all knowing.

We are now to look at everything from the standpoint of mind only and bend all our energies to the true understanding of it. We are to study the showing forth of mid from seeming darkness to light; from seeming nothingness to existence; from seeming void to life; from seeming ignorance to knowledge.

In order to do so, we must study creation. In creation we all came forth from this Divine Mind and are still one with It.

We as mind came forth from the Infinite Mind are one with our Origin. We came forth to show what real Mind is.

When we speak Truth concerning our Origin we are as light shining in darkness. When we speak other than Truth it is keeping the light of True Mind from coming forth. "Let there be light." "The earth was without form and void."

The Real Mind was made in the image or form of God, so the earth mind was without form. The Mind that is God is the only Real Mind, so the earth mind was null and void, pure nothingness of ignorance of the Real Mind and its Powers.

We must interpret the Scriptures according to knowledge of the God-Mind, and for mind.

In mind lore, "waters" means conscious thoughts, and Spirit means word and Life for, He who taught us of the Scriptures and of God, said, "My words are Spirit and they are Life."

So we understand "The Spirit of God moved across the face of the waters" to mean that the word and Life of God move across our thoughts to "Let there be light" in our mind and clear away the earth ways of thinking, replacing them by words of Truth.

Knowing the True Mind we easily find what those earth ideas are that are void of reality and Truth and have not brought the health and peace that are born of God from whom we came forth.

Jesus said, "Search the Scriptures" and they say "A man's word is his only burden." Then if we would be rid of our burdens we must drop our words and take the word of God that moves across our thoughts, or mind, find its hidden or spiritual meaning and let it swell and flow through all our thoughts until they are one with it; until we are conscious of no others. Then we shall begin to comprehend the True Mind which the race has been so ignorant of, or Truth itself.

We have learned of God or the foundation of Being as our first step in the knowledge of Mind and Law. The second step is to know why we have not understood our creation heretofore and what this darkness called ignorance is, from which we must emerge into Light or understanding of Mind.

We have been assured that "If ye know Truth the Truth shall make you free."

Not only did Jesus say this, but all the wise of earth have agreed in saying that there is Truth somewhere which if found would make men free.

Free from what?

Is it not the whole race in bondage to something?

Either to some habit or appetite or to the effect of some disposition or sin in others, or to some unpleasant environment by which it is fettered; kept from rising as upon the wings of the morning to light and happiness?

Perhaps it is some secret thought, or some thought or act of cruelty in another.

All, all have something.

These fetters must be struck off; hammered at if necessary till they break asunder and let us free..

How?

By following the teaching of all the wise. By denying the power over us of flesh and fleshly ways.

We are encased in a shell of materialism which encloses us as closely as the shell of a bivalve does its originator.

The oyster made its shell and so have we made ours.

One who has opened and oyster knows that there is a certain way to do it easily and with out trouble, so that the shell yields at once liberating its inmate to light. If the right way is not understood, the shell can be hammered till it breaks all to pieces and leaves the oyster free.

We have both knife and hammer. We can sharpen the knife and find the place in our shell to open and show us the Truth that sets free, or we may slowly hammer at each part of it, breaking it by piecemeal until we are freed from it and are forced to acknowledge Truth.

If we are in fetters we cannot walk. If we wear goggles we cannot see. So if we would be free indeed we must throw off the shackles which blind and bind us.

A great army of wise students have declared that all that we see is but a "shadow system," that there is a hidden meaning to everything, for which we must search if we would know the divine idea of creation and the design of our own life.

The scriptures must be searched to find their inner meaning, and for nineteen hundred years many and varied have been the interpretations of them; for there are said to be one thousand different religions and sects, and of these there are but nine that do not use the Bible as their guide and reference. This excludes the Jews who use but a part of it.

Then there must be nearly one thousand interpretations of the meaning of Scripture with some shade of difference, and many people in each sect differ in their private opinions of the significance of its words.

Thus as we progress in our study of the showing forth

of Mind we find that the whole race has held false ideas concerning its creation and progression, which have caused the bondage under which we all labor and which we must be rid of if we would understand the hidden or spiritual meaning of the words that are life, or the Truth that constitutes freedom.

If we seek for light on any subject whatever we are sure to find it, for they who truly seek *shall* find. That is the Law. The very act of seeking proves that there is something to be found that will satisfy.

Then we must seek for this Truth in earnest and with persistence and we shall be rewarded. All religions hold a germ of Truth, and we will take it wherever we find it.

One religion says that it is only by dropping material thoughts that we are awake to divine things, or have spiritual understanding.

All religions say that spirituality brings peace and health. Spirituality is knowledge of absolute Truth.

The wisest teachers and students of material things own, that with all their knowledge, they really know nothing. They have studied enough to find out that their knowledge profiteth nothing, does not help in the least to lift them out of bondage.

All great teachers in the world have taught that material transactions are only symbolic of the divine Reality, and that material creations are but typical of the spiritual creations.

Then the spiritual is the true, and material transactions and thoughts are what we are to drop, or the false ideas held by the race, that cause the bondage.

What are they and how shall we be rid of them? Where shall we seek for this spirituality and for a knowledge of our false ideas that hinder its shining forth?

All great teachers have said that Truth can only be found by leaving material seeking and doing. All have taught that Soul was the only reality and have denied the importance of material things.

Donnelly says, "The present age has entered upon a new era; it has added a series of wonderful inventions to the Atlantean list; it has subjugated steam and electricity to the use of man. And its work has but commenced; it will continue until it lifts man to a plane as much higher than the present as the present is above the barbaric condition."

This sounds prophetic of the new dispensation-of Mind.

The greatest teacher of all said, "flesh profiteth nothing: it is the spirit that quickeneth."

We must seek in His words the enlightenment we need, for He also said, "My words are spirit and life." He said, "judge not according to appearance," and we have been taught by all that material and fleshly things are only an appearance, a delusion, and not the reality.

When James spoke of the life of flesh he called it, "A vapor that appeareth for a little time and then vanisheth away."

Now, if we are to follow the teachings of Jesus, we shall find something more to do than simply believing His words. We must *follow* Him, as He said, and He told just how to follow Him.

"If any man will come after me let him deny himself,"

As he said these words in reproof of thinking too much of fleshly things and ways, He must have meant deny material things- the appearance.

We learned in the first lesson that the life principle is God, and that God is the only substance in the universe and this substance is Spirit. Then Spirit is the only reality and what we call matter is not real at all.

This proves that the self we are to deny in order to follow Jesus, is the fleshly or material self and all things pertaining to matter. Deny that they are true or have any power at all.

Denial is not new. It is as old as creation and was the first lesson taught by God to man, according to Genesis. He commanded them not to gratify their fleshly appetite, but as they did not obey the command of denial, "eat not" they were in bondage to flesh thereby losing the inheritance of the garden of truth or happiness. They listened to thoughts of sense for "The serpent is the principle of sensuous thought."

Thus, God finished the work called "Very Good" by inculcating the rejection of evil.

All the prophets taught denial of fleshly ways and so did the apostles. All religions teachers taught that the way to happiness was by denying fleshly appetites and habits, or the life of the senses, as that was not the true life.

Sometimes the effect of this teaching was such an excess of denial that the material self was scourged and tortured in order to bring the spiritual life and self uppermost, and people hid themselves away from the sight of material things.

All this shows that matter had a very strong hold upon them and they had not learned its unreality. They fled from it as from a powerful reality. They did not grasp the idea of denial meant by Jesus-the saving word of denial.

Denial is one of the factors used in solving the problem of life and we can prove whether the factor is correct or not at each step of the way, for if we use denial properly it rids us of those false ideas, leaving us free. Then denial must prepare the way for the truth that sets free.

These false ideas that have been like darkness to our earth mind are the errors spoken of in the first lesson which must be erased before our life problem will be correctly solved.

They are beliefs that are not true and while untrue are held the true cannot show forth. Until the errors are erased we are not able to know the right figures in any problem.

The first statement of our problem is that God is the only Substance, the only Presence, the only Power in the universe.

Now the first error made in trying to solve the problem of life is that there is another power and presence, named evil.

It is not strange that the race did not once see the utter impossibility of such an idea?

All own that God is Good, and the Omnipresence of Good annihilates the idea of any other presence in the universe. The omnipotence of Good repudiates the idea of any of other power.

All who have this error have not got the right answer to their problem because they have never found the Truth that freed them from bondage; never found the satisfaction that we called the answer.

Then if we are seeking Truth we must erase this error by denying that there is any evil at all anywhere. If we have found Truth and the right factor when we say "there is no evil," it will prove itself true and right by making us free from evil. Wherever we speak the words, evil will cease to be.

Bad tempers will fall away, evil deeds stop, lies turn to truth, anger and hate to love, injustice to justice and sorrow to joy.

Does it not sound true to say that if God or Good is everywhere there is no room for evil? If we say it and it makes us free from evil that proves it to be Truth.

What is evil?

It is sin, sickness and death.

Is it not good news that they are not true, that they do not exist, that we need not have them come near us? Is this an hard doctrine? It is at least a pleasant one if true, and we can easily prove whether it is true or not.

So potent is Truth that even saying its words over and over when we do not quite understand or believe them, will bring freedom to us, but as we grow to believe, their power is more and more apparent to us.

Each human being really believes that there is somewhere in the universe good for him and all his striving is for the purpose of obtaining it. He thinks he *ought* to have it and that in it will be no mixture of evil. But we have been taught to smother any such hope of supreme good as for us in this world.

It is often said that it makes no difference what we believe if we are only in earnest.

But it does make a vast difference for the race has believed in evil as a great power, a power equal to God, ever since the world began. Has it made no difference? Have they been happy and well and strong and good?

No. The race has never known real health and strength and life, for they are eternal, and people have gone through weakness and sickness down to death at the rate of millions per minute of all these thousands of years.

To believe is to serve, and to serve is to worship, so it makes all difference imaginable what we believe in, for to worship more than one God is against the Law, and if we believe in a power of equal to God, we worship another God, an evil God. "Ye shall have no other God but me" – "I Am the Lord your God."

This God who thus speaks is The Good. We have worshiped another power, which is idolatry, and have had our reward. Now let us hurl this false God from its throne and acknowledge only the True One forevermore.

How shall we displace the belief in, or worship of evil?

By denial of its reality, power and truth. There is no other way. It may require hard work, but so it would to remove any chains that bound us. Continued effort will do anything.

This false God that we have made, has had a far reaching influence and we have much to undo, for under the head of evil there are five beliefs that tend to death instead of life.

We have believed that material life has substance. Have we not spoken of hills as being everlasting when the truth is, they are being ceaselessly washed into sea?

We speak of earth as being "terra firma" when there is really nothing firm or solid about it, for earth and sea are ever changing places.

How can we call earth "solid materials" when all its particles are always going through some change and becoming something else? We speak of flesh as solid and there is no solidity in it. It also changes rapidly. All things of earth-materialthings-are fleeting, transient, perishable; then how could we think of them as substance?

We have been told often that they are all but shadows of the hidden reality, "a shadow system gathered round our Me" and that the fleshly man is "like a shadow that declineth, and withereth like grass."

We have thought we believed all this and yet have called matter real, called it substance.

Substance must be eternal; that is the test. There is nothing eternal but Spirit-God-therefore God is the only Substance. Spirit is the only Reality.

This is Truth and we must reject all else. There is no reality in matter. *There is no matter.*

Speak the true words and watch the result; look for proof of their truth. Thousands are proving them true, for where they are spoken things of matter pass from view like the pictures of a magic lantern.

The hard tumor vanishes like a dream that it was; swellings are gone at a word; sickness comes no more; sorrows are found to be nothing; material conditions drop away, showing their unreality. The reality coming to view as the untrue conditions fade away.

The next belief held by the race, that is an error, is that what we call matter has life, sensation or intelligence. This is wholly untrue.

Spirit is All; then matter is nothing and nothing cannot feel or know anything. Life is only the enduring in Substance, in Spirit.

If we would see the results of truth we must deny this error also and declare there is no life, intelligence or sensation in matter, for matter does not really exist; it is nothing.

Those who thus deny have no more fear of cold or heat; of earthquake, famine or pestilence for they are but the outcome of false beliefs.

They no longer sorrow because of death for they know their loved ones live eternally in the bosom of the Infinite Father where we all abide, and that in his loving care is no separation. His Arms are sufficient to hold all within their embrace.

They learn that knowledge is of and from God, and that all have access to it which makes the striving for book lore of secondary importance. Real knowledge is free, without money and without price. We have only to hide our faces and listen.

They find the Substance of all things lovely, proving how unsatisfying are all things of the earth mind, houses, lands, honors or anything that has seemed beautiful and desirable.

No matter how much scorn and rejection there may be of this Truth, wherever it is spoken the desolate shall rejoice, the deserted be comforted, the poor find plenty and those of no ability be found to have good judgment and capability in the affairs of life.

Spirit is the only Power. It has the only sight, the only hearing, the only feeling.

Why did we give those faculties to flesh when we are told that "flesh profiteth nothing?"

Another error is in believing there can be sin, sickness and death for the child of God. God never made or ordained such things, for God is Spirit, and His creations are only Spirit. can Spirit be sick or sin?

Spirit and matter have nothing to do with each other, and it is our wandering from Spirit that brought upon us such seemings. We have created these things by calling them true, by allowing our thoughts to dwell upon the unreal and calling it real.

Now, we must deny them and say there is no sin, sickness or death.

When these words are spoken the cruel are powerless, the sensual find no more pleasure in the senses, the sick rise up strong and well, the dying feel renewed life rush in every vein, stirring every fiber of the earthly frame till his very soul cries out, *I am alive.* It is the breath of God, the "breath of life that makes him a living soul," the only creation.

We must let go our earth ideas, or ideas of the earth mind, for it is nor the real Mind. There is but one Mind and that is God. We are creations of that Mind and are one with It, then our thoughts must be life unto His thoughts, and true and real.

God is ALL and God is Good. Only the Good is true, for Good is the only Substance, the only Life, the only Intelligence, the only Power and only Spirit.

Evil is not, never was and never can be a power or a principle. This is the denial Jesus made and taught-that evil is not reality, for God (Good) is ALL.

These are the rejections we are to make in order to see all former things pass away and all things become as new.

In my idea of Good there is no mixture of evil. There can be no evil in Spirit, Christ, Reality.

There is no matter in Truth, Life, Love.

There is no absence of Life anywhere.

Sin, sickness and death are not Realities, but dreams.

There is no sensation in what we call matter. Spirit hears, sees, feels, and can hear, see, feel only good.

There is nothing to hate anywhere, for *All is Love.*

# NOTES

# NOTES

CHAPTER III.

_____

## Necessary Affirmations.

_____

In the second lesson we said that our aim in this study, is systematic knowledge of mind. System is order, and we know that "Order is heaven's first law." Things that are done in order are done by degrees, by steps.

Our first step was to find what the Principle of all Life is. That is the Principle by which we are to solve the problem of our own life and make of it what was purpose of creation.

After we know the Principle we want rules to work with and by. It is rules of mind that we are to know.

The second step we found was to erase all errors heretofore made that had brought the wrong answer to us. That is done by denial of the untrue and unreal.

The third step then is necessarily to find something to lean upon after the old props have been taken away; something substantial if the old methods were all wrong.

The work we are to do is all of the mind and is done by mind, so it must be a work of thinking.

As our errors were of thought we must find in what right thinking consists. The study of mind and its modes of thought must be pursued through reasoning from sure premises to a clear, convincing conclusion.

Our first premise is, that God or Good is all there is in the universe and is Spirit; thus the second and a natural sequence is that there can be no evil where Good reigns, and no matter where Spirit is all.

The second step was a rejection of all claims outside of the Good. This rejection or denial is an important step in mind culture because it cleanses the mind of all impurities, or wrong thoughts, -thrusts out the tares and prepares the soil for seed that it may grown to complete fruitage.

To plant the seed is the third step. We have thrown off the darkness of false beliefs and must now admit the light of right thoughts. We have cleansed the mind, unclothed it of falsity, we must now put on the fresh clean clothing of true statements.

We have erased the errors in our problem and must put down the correct propositions that will give the answer we desire, the true one. We have cast out the deaf and dumb earth mind-error-by the fasting of denial, and are now ready for the prayer of affirming the Truth, for "This kind goeth not out but by prayer and fasting."

Belief in evil is cast out by fasting or denial, and Truth is established in our mind upon a firm basis by the prayer of affirmation. For prayer is simply affirming or declaring what is true, for Jesus said, "Pray as if he had already received." It is thanking God for all the blessings He has already bestowed. When we do this they begin to show forth our sight.

We are studying the creation by Mind-God; of mind in its manifestation of the reality of its creation as a thought of the Creator. Denying the void and formless to prove the image of its Creator, from the "Darkness upon the face of the deep" to the "Let there be light."

"And God divided the light from the darkness." We proceed to do the same; to follow the order He established in creating, in our recreating or unfolding of our own perfect mind.

We banished the darkness of error that the light might enter, for darkness is only the light unacknowledged.

We are now ready for the third step; ready to see the light as good, for the statement of creation is, "And God saw the light that it was good."

In our study, "Let there be light" means that we must make every effort to dispel darkness, by seeking light. Use every exertion to find the truth that frees us from thraldom.

Denials alone do not bring light or freedom, for it is truth that is to free and denial is simply to cleanse from error, make ready for the truth that frees.

Denials cleanse and fit for the fresh garment of truth but do not clothe us in it, do not put it on for us. We are cleansed of thoughts of error.

Thoughts of Truth will clothe our mind with robes of righteousness or right thinking. Our new robes are right thoughts, right words, and the words of God are the only right words. When we have found these words we shall be in the light and find that it is indeed "Good."

What are these words that are so potent to change all our life; all our ways of thinking and acting, and where shall we find them?

They are the words of Jesus Christ and by them He wrought seeming miracles. As people did not understand His words so they did not know the power in them when spoken, and looked upon his works as miraculous. There is a law in regard to words and this law He obeyed and brought forth works in accordance therewith.

Any one who knows the law can do the same. He claimed nothing especially for himself. It was His Father who did the works and the same Father will do the same works for us, through us, *if* we obey the *law* and use the words.

No other teaching has ever taken away sickness, pain and trouble from human experience, and no other can do it.

The reason the doctrine of Jesus has not always done this when preached is because those who taught it, taught that we must wait until some future time to be free from these things; that they are our lot and portion now and here.

It is true that "In the world ye shall have tribulation," but we should not be in the world but in heaven, for Jesus said, "The kingdom of heaven is within," and we can choose which kingdom we will have within. Tribulation is only for the earth mind and we must rise above earth into our God-created being; into the kingdom prepared for us before the foundation of the world.

Jesus' teaching and works were orderly or according to law and we will follow his footsteps in their order. Teaching Spiritual Law is only teaching the doctrine and explaining the miracles of Jesus Christ.

Jesus taught to deny over and over, saying "Man shall not live by bread alone." "Lay not up for yourselves treasures upon earth." "Take no thought what ye shall eat or drink." "Judge not." "Tempt not the Lord."

"The flesh profiteth nothing." "If any man will come after me let him deny himself." "Resist the devil."

The sermon on the mount is full of declarations

concerning the kingdom of God and how to enter therein, and is concluded by the declaration, "He that doeth the will of my Father shall enter into the kingdom of heaven."

As a race we have not entered into the kingdom of heaven, but have been content to put off our entrance therein to some far off time and place. This only proves that we have not done the will of the Father or we should have found His kingdom within us.

How content we have been to wait and suffer and go down through the grave to find heaven when it has been right here very near all the time.

Why have we been thus content?

Has it been easier to bear suffering and pain than to obey the law of love to all men?

Has it been easier to bear trouble than to give up selfishness, envy, hatred and malice?

Has it been easier to look upon death and accidents than to be temperate in all things, than to control the passions?

Has it been easier to be weak and feeble than to be just and honest to all men?

Has it been easier to have stiff joints and lame back and limbs than to be pure in thought, word and deed?

Has it been easier to have and witness disease and death than to be strong and firm in principle?

Is it easier to live in sin and be forgiven, being rewarded for our many repentances at some future time, than to obey the will of God at once?

To do the will of the Father perfectly requires some exertion on our part. The casting aside of habits, prejudices, sins that are dear, and losing opportunities to better our earthly conditions.

We are even more indolent than those people of the Eastern Hemisphere who deny even their lives away and lie upon the ground all the time or bury themselves beneath it in order to find a heaven of perfect stillness. They at least try to find their heaven now.

We have been willing to postpone ours indefinitely for the sake of living in the senses, even if we do suffer. It has seemed harder to do the will of God than to suffer.

We have not been willing to think right thoughts, for Jesus plainly taught them. Have they been followed when most and best understood? No.

People have always known that the will of God is to be just, but they have said, "O, it is impossible to be strictly just and honest in business dealings and have success, for everyone cheats and we only obey the law of self preservation."

It is too hard to obey "Thou shalt not steal," and so much easier to swallow quinine and mercury.

People have always known that the will of God is to "Love thy neighbor as thyself," and yet have hated and cruelly entreated others upon slightest provocation.

It was too difficult to obey "Thou shalt do no murder" and would be so lowering to pride to allow an insult to go unpunished and unresented. "He that hateth his brother is a murderer in his heart."

Who can resist the speech or look of contempt or derision at some act or word of another, or the temptation to roll the sweet morsel gossip under the tongue? Who withholds the unkind criticism upon acts, looks, and words of others?

O, it is altogether too hard to obey "Thou shalt not bear false witness." It is far easier to bear poverty or trouble than to think no evil.

It is so much easier to believe in a gigantic power stalking through the world, and to make it responsible for all our misdeeds and wrong thoughts, even to believe that the God we say we worship made this power, exactly opposed to His own, than to rise up in our might and obey the first command of all, "Thou shalt have no other God but me."

It is to hard to have a God that is All Good and no other, because if we do his will, every single thought we have must be good, just, gentle and loving.

Is it not very easy to understand that our own thoughts have made all our misery?

God never made misery for he pronounced all he made "very good."

It is the earth thoughts that tend to death. "Turn ye, for why will ye die?"

We must do the will of the Father in order to enter the kingdom. We must do the will if we would prove the doctrine. We must do the will if we would find satisfactory Life in the Truth that will make us free. Do the will in thought as well as in word and act.

It has been said and taught as a truth that "thoughts are things." Thought is an evidence of the state of mind of the thinker.

Jesus told of nine different blessings that the kingdom of Heaven confers and seven of them are the rewards of states of mind. All of the greatest teachers of the world have emphasized strongly right thinking as a prime time factor in correct living and the way to attain happiness.

The man called the wisest who ever live said, "In the way of righteousness is life; and in the pathway thereof there is no death."

"He that speaketh truth showeth forth righteousness."

"The lip of truth shall be established forever." "The tongue of the wise is health."

The Jewish Rabbis tell us that the true significance of righteousness is "right thinking." Does it not sound reasonable, for certainly right thoughts will produce right speech and right action.

When Solomon's words are thus interpreted how plainly they make the path in which we are to walk.

In the way of right thought is life. Spoken Truth is right thought and shall be established forever. If the speech of the wise is health surely he is wise who thinks rightly.

Is it not easy to see why we have not had health, happiness and life eternal here and now?

We have not thought right.

As there are words that cleanse the mind, so there are words that satisfy, clothe, rejoice and fill the mind with right thoughts. These are the words of only absolute Truth and they have wonderful effect and power upon those who speak them and upon all those around about them.

These powerful words or statements have been made by all the good and great of the world. They are the truth concerning God. Whoever has spoken them has had wonderful experiences.

Paul was "caught up into paradise and heard unspeakable words not lawful for a man to utter," by speaking them. Many have risen to undreamed of power by their use. Some have passed through fire unharmed, others through floods in safety.

These words of truth are called affirmations, and follow the denials in the order in which we train the mind to systematic knowledge.

First the nay, nay to the unreal and untrue called evil, then the yea, yea to the Real, True and Good ever present, brings the "light that was good," and is good forever, about us and through us, filling us with joy enduring and complete.

The true words concerning God are that God is the All Good and is present in all places. There is no point of space where he is not. God is Life eternal, Truth unvarying, Love unfailing, Substance unchangeable, Intelligence indisputable.

Omnipresence, or all presence-Omnipotence, or All Power-Omniscience, or All Knowledge.

These are true words. When we speak them do we know what we are saying? When we make a true statement it proves that the opposite is not true at all. Then if God is All Life and everywhere present, this Life cannot be absent or interrupted, or permit us to know death. Life Itself, the Omnipotent Life, is eternal can *not* change. So if we are alive to-day we are alive forever.

If we have loved ones that were alive once, they are alive now, even though our physical eyes do not behold what we have called their forms. In Omnipresence there can be no absence, then the dear ones are present with us ever and always. We do not at all mean that there is any material manifestation of those who have gone on, or any vision of them. Remember that we deny matter in toto. There is only Spirit and we are dealing with the science of Spirit and its explanations.

Scientific understanding of Spirit is the highest attainment of spirituality, but not in the least spiritual-*ism*, for we repeat knowledge of Spirit rejects the belief in material manifestations, does not even recognize matter of flesh, has nothing to do with physical sense or sight.

There is an inner seeing that is keener, clearer than physical sight. Physical sight is but a shadow of the real sight.

The blind know their friends by touch, by feeling, by intuition, and in like manner we can feel the presence of all created beings, for all are one with the Infinite Father, are one in Him. Not one ever leaves His loving arms that are as high and deep and broad as the universe. Life is deathless eternity. It is the Principle of Being and Principle never changes, cannot be extinguished.

God is Truth. Is there anything that we can conceive of greater, higher, more powerful than Truth? In Truth "is no variableness, neither shadow of turning."

It is something upon which we can rely, in which we can trust, in which we rest as the child rests in its mother's arms, and where we can find repose. It is the rock that is the firm foundation for all our hopes, and though winds of adversity, floods of trouble, a rain of persecution should beat about us, if we are anchored to Truth none of them can or will prevail or can shake us, for we are founded upon the rock of Truth. It is the rock of our salvation upon which our feet are firmly and immovably planted.

It is the haven into which we may steer our storm-tossed boat of human experience to find a safe harbor.

It is like being upon a bridge high above the rushing river below, safe from the raging waters. Mortal transactions are like the river flowing along under the bridge where we stand so high above, but they cannot move us, for the bridge of Truth is under our feet.

Human experiences are generally more easily comprehended than abstract truths. Then let us think of one who is dear and in whose love we trust. Do we not rely upon his word implicitly, would we not sooner think of doubting self than him? Would we not willingly place our very life in his power, knowing that he would do the best in all ways for us? If life or character or honor was threatened would we not trust to his defense, nothing doubting? Is there not a feeling of safety, protection, confidence, repose and perfect calm in his presence?

Do we not feel as if he was a power that was reliable and unchangeable, and that we could stake our all upon his fidelity, constancy and kindness? Can we ask more than such a friend as this? Is there greater happiness upon earth?

Is he not a human representation of the love that is God? If a human creation can be all this, what must God be? Can we not raise our ideas from finite to Infinite, lift our thoughts from human to divine?

The Truth that is God is all this and more, yes, more than we can even imagine, but the greater our efforts to understand and the more we trust what we do comprehend, the higher the conception of Infinite Truth will be.

To look thus to Truth with trust is to speak Truth, and its words are life, health and wisdom to all who speak them. Truth is the God who is a "present help"-the God who is Omnipresent Good to the exclusion of any other force whatever.

God is Love. Is there anything more satisfying than love? Is it not quite true that the dinner of herbs is better with one we love than the stalled ox where love is unknown or where unkindness and strife are rife? If we have all the material things that money can procure, with a palace for a home, friends who praise or flatter, sumptuous fare, fine clothing and every luxury, are we happy or content if these are shared with one we cannot love?

It is an old saying that "love flies out of the window when poverty comes in at the door," but it is not true, for "love endureth all things." Anything is enjoyable if only shared by genuine love. It is not love at all that can be changed by circumstances.

Real love is like that of a mother for her child. Who forgiveth all iniquity like a mother? Who supplies all wants as a mother does for her child? Who forestalls all needs like the true mother? Who comforts in sorrow, soothes away pain by her touch, quiets all fear, charms away vexation or temper, trouble or remorse by her gentle admonition, and holds to her heart though all the world forsake or treat with contempt? Who *can* be like a mother or who could fill her place?

Is there one?

Yes, God, for God is Love Itself, and the mother's love is but one manifestation of Infinite Love. The love that is God is as much greater than any we know of in human beings as perfection is above what we call sin.

In love there is strength, and it brings physical strength for we become so absorbed in the sentiment and in ministering to the object of love that we entirely forget and ignore self thus letting the physical take care of itself, which is the surest way to be well.

In love is vitality, for it supplies an aim, an object upon which to expend all our energies. In love is the highest content, the most complete happiness, the most entire satisfaction, the deepest joy, that the heart of man can know in earth life.

When we say God is Love we mean the comfort, supply, patience, endurance, mercy, kindness, and gentleness of a mother, but in a supreme sense, for God is both Father and Mother.

We mean the tenderness and care of a husband only supreme, for "Thy Maker is thy husband."

We mean the supreme persistence, attention and endurance of a lover, for the Lord said, "Yea, I have loved thee with an everlasting love; therefore with loving kindness have I drawn thee." God is a lover, ever near and constant, all enduring, "who crowneth us with mercy and loving kindness."

When we know this Supreme Love, we find that those whom we love are nearer and dearer, for all "Our loves in higher love endure."

Our friendships are an illustration of our capability and readiness to reach Supreme Love and understand it, and of our progress toward it, for if we take notice of the kind and quality of those we draw to us and to whom we are attracted we shall find that as we approach the understanding of true, real love, each true friend that we have is better and dearer to us than former friends.

The true explanation is we are more fully awake to a higher expression of love. The real self is showing forth.

God is Substance. Is not substance a word that conveys a feeling of security as if we had something to stand upon that could never change, something to cling to with a feeling of sure protection? A fortress in which to hide from all the battles of mortality and upon whose battlements we may stand with perfect safety, looking down upon the world of seeming called matter and evil with calmness and peace?

God is Spirit, thus Spirit is the Substance and is so close to us that we not only lean upon It but we are one with It, for Spirit is our Creator, Supporter and Preserver.

When we say that Spirit is the only Substance, matter loses its hold for we are so folded round safety, strength and peace that we cease from our vain striving, and rest upon the "Height where lies repose." Things of flesh cannot reach us with their changing currents and restless tides, for our bulwark is high and strong and a sure defense. Though we sail far out upon the Infinite we have safe and sure guidance and always a firm resting place for our feet. *God* is our Substance.

God is Intelligence. To say this will find our mind with true wisdom, excluding the knowledge that is "Foolishness with God."

We have only knowledge that profiteth, and show it forth in our own words and thoughts. We can say "I think Thy thoughts after Thee, O God." And we are taught by this wisdom that we are the thought, the idea, the creation of God and in him "live and move and have our being." Then we know that all our efforts are unnecessary, for God works through us to will and to do. We can lay down our oars. God does all through us and for us an in us. It is His Life that we live, His speech that we speak, His thoughts that we think, His work that is done through us. We have nothing to do but simply let it *be* done. "Thy will be done."

Over the entrance of a temple in Greece was placed the words "Know Thyself." This was the motto of Solon, one of the seven sages, and there is none that is better adapted to our needs. To know Self is to know our origin, for we must know from whence we came and how, in order to understand Self.

In studying mind we find that the origin of all creation is Mind, or Spirit, called God or First Cause.

Anaxagoras was the first philosopher who attributed the beginning and ordering of the world to a pure unadulterated intelligence.

Plutarch says that for this reason Anaxagoras was called Nous.

Nous means mind or intelligence so the people spoke better than they knew when they called the one who discovered that mind was the universal power, by the same name given to that Power, or Mind. They unconsciously recognized the oneness of man and God or the origin of man.

As the Cause of all things-God-is Spirit, His creations must be Spirit, because Spirit is the only Substance from which to create. They must be Intelligence because from Intelligence. They must be Mind because of Mind. They must reflect, manifest or show forth all that their creator is, for He made man in his own show forth all that their creator is, for He made man in his own image and likeness.

We then know Self for we are like Him who made us. We are Mind, Spirit, Intelligence, Substance, Goodness, Wisdom, Strength and Holiness. This is the real Self of us-Spirit.

"By their fruits ye shall know them." By our works we prove ourselves children of the good and co-workers with him to rescue the world from sin, sickness and death by our healing, loving, efficient thoughts.

As His creations we are governed only by His Law, love only His Law, till we know there is no other. Then, we cannot know sin, for to do good is not only our privilege but our pleasure and joy. We have no desire to sin. It is hateful to us.

If we know not sin, neither can we know death, for "by sin came death." Not only do we not sin, but sin cannot stay near us. We are a silent protest against it and people who are near us forsake their sins. Our words of Truth put sin away.

If we say we cannot sin we do not mean anything like the doctrine of sanctification, which was that the elect where beyond the power to sin so that no matter what they did, their doing it made it right in the sight of God. When we say we cannot sin we do not wish to convey any idea of a license to sin, or that we can do just as we please. (Humanly speaking).

O, no; our God is not at all like that. He never connives at sin. If we sin we are not with Him, do not know Him at all. Of course He is always present but knows us not, for He cannot draw any nearer to us. It is for us to draw near to Him in spirit and in truth.

Matter and falsehood, or sin, are never near Him, so we must leave them in order to find God. God does not see sin, does not know sin, for God is Spirit *only* and Spirit knows nothing of flesh. It is only in Spirit that we approach or know God. And Spirit cannot sin, so when we live only in spirit we cannot sin. "He beholdeth not iniquity."

When we wake to the life of Spirit we find it so far beyond flesh and its ways that we love it only and hate and forsake sin, till we behold not iniquity. It becomes so foreign to our nature that we shun all tendency to it even in thought.

Speaking or affirming the Truth brings us so near to God that we love His Law and Love only the good. Then sin no more abounds in us for we are awake to righteousness, awake to Spirit. We no longer fear death and when fear is gone sickness is also gone, for fear is the great promoter of sickness and death.

To speak the affirmations of the Law of Spirit will change all our world to our vision, though no one else may behold the change. We have real sight, or insight, to see that things of earth are nothing worth.

Things that once vexed us vex us no more for they now seem insignificant. Things that once pleased us please us no more for we now know the true from the false, we know pure gold from the counterfeit coin. Things that we once desired we no longer wish for.

Material things have vanished from our horizon. We know them no more. We breathe a divine air and are thus enabled to see the divine meaning of all things. We know that only the Good is true and that Good is all there is to know.

Many people feel discouraged in studying this Law because so many who have learned seemingly all they can of it still have sickness and trouble in their homes and themselves just like other people.

Learning a theory however beautiful is but a small part of the work. We may learn all the notes on the keyboard of a piano by name, and all the notes of the staff with those above and below ever so perfectly; we may then learn all that can be told about the quality and quantity and value of notes, rests, sharps, flats and chords. Can we then play the simplest of Beethoven's sonatas or even the simplest exercise well? No.

We have not made our knowledge practical. No matter what or how much we learn, we must practice all we have learned as we go on at each step.

Scientific Law is like everything else and must be used to be truly known. We can only know the doctrine by doing the will, which is to live it, practice its rules every instant.

As we try to do this we find one old belief in evil after another to be gotten rid of. It seems like a game of ten pins; beliefs being set up in array like the pins, and we roll our ball of denial at each one, sometimes hitting others. We knock down all we can think of when lo, there are more set up, and we must go on knocking down.

It is not always easy but neither is work of any kind easy, and persistent effort is all that wins in anything whatever. The results are great and all that is requisite is to "watch and pray."

Praying is to repeat the affirmations, or True words. They are, God is Life; God is Truth; God is Love; God is Substance; God is Intelligence.

God is Omnipresence, therefore Life, Love, Truth, Substance and Intelligence are in all places alike and are the birthright of each.

God is Omnipotence, so the All Power is Life, Truth, Love, Substance, Intelligence, which totally excludes death, falsity, hatred, changeableness.

God is Omniscience, then All Wisdom is everywhere and no one can be foolish or ignorant.

The more we declare, affirm, these statements, the more quickly we shall see and feel their power to change us and all around us. When they are received into the heart we rejoice in knowing, and continually say, "I am Spirit and one with the Infinite Spirit. I partake of and am one with Strength, Health, Peace, Wisdom. God works through me to will and to do all things. I am governed by the Law of God and know neither sin, sickness nor death. I am one with God.

# NOTES

# NOTES

# CHAPTER IV. 57

## Faith.

We have taken three steps in our study of mind or search for truth. We have found that the Principle of Life is Good and is Spirit, and we have found of what Good is composed and where Spirit is.

We have discovered the laws by which this Principle works and how to apply them to our own life problem in order to solve it correctly. The next step must be one of decision each for himself.

Do we accept all this as reasonable and are we willing to obey these rules?

Do we believe that these statements are statement of truth and the very truth that we want? Do we believe that they are The Truth that will save us from all that has heretofore been distressing and hard to endure?

Does our mind assent to these propositions and accept them as true?

This is the important question now. Assent is faith and if we have not the belief that is faith we can go no farther in our study, and the rest will be simply a hearing of the outer ears.

Real study is with the mind and tends to understanding of The Mind, or Spirit, or spiritual understanding which is real or true knowledge. As we approach this knowledge we begin to see that all that we have before called knowledge profiteth nothing, and must be left behind us in our onward progress must be recognized as only the shadow of what is true.

Matter cannot take cognizance of Spirit, therefore, as we understand Spirit and its ways, we know that we have been following after shadows.

This progress seems necessarily slow. If we were in a dark room and were suddenly taken out into the strong sunlight it would blind us. The light would be too great.

Ignorance of Spirit is a darkness of the mind. All things must be done in order as we step forth into the light.

This idea of the real knowledge and its semblance, is very old, for Plato said, "In the world of knowledge the idea of good is last seen and with difficulty, but when seen is inferred to be the author of good and right-parent of the Lord of light in this world and of truth and understanding in the other."

He compared human beings to captives in a cave 'who see nothing but the shadows which the fire throws on the wall of the cave; to these they give names and if we add an echo which returns from the wall voices will seem to proceed from the shadows. Suppose now that you turn the people and show them that the shadows are cast by images will they believe it? Suppose they are dragged up a steep and rugged ascent into the presence of the sun, will not their eyes be darkened with the excess of light? Sometime will pass before they get the habit of perceiving at all, but when at length they do behold the sun in his own proper place as he is how they will rejoice in passing from darkness to light: how worthless to them will seem the honors and glories of the den or cave out of which they came."

He explains that he means the cave to represent the world of sight, the sun the fire, and the way upward the way of knowledge.

Thus we see that this doctrine of spiritual knowledge the unreality of material things was taught five hundred years before Christ. It has been called metaphysics. When Berkeley taught it people called it idealism. Emerson taught it and was called a transcendentalist.

Well, heaven *is* transcendental, ideas are realities and metaphysics the plane upon which we stand in order to reach true knowledge.

We now find that these ideas held so long ago are good sense and sound reasoning, and when held to, bring the best and happiest results.

Plato was quite right, the world of sight, or sense, *is* a cave in which we are blinded to the real and true. Out of this we must come and leave the shadows on the wall, which are the beliefs in mortal things as being real or as having any pleasure in them.

If at first we do not see or believe this, we must obey the ruses, use denial and affirmation persistently till the faith comes. We must "do the will" first then the faith in the doctrine as true will come.

Faith does not come without effort. We cannot find Substance unless we seek for it, and faith is the substance of things hoped for.

We have always hoped for health and happiness. If we persist in the use of our rules we find health and happiness, and then faith in the Principle must be ours.

Our attitude must be "not faithless but believing," that is, willing to believe and not opposing the statements.

Drummond says that "the use of faith is to connect the soul with God, and the use of being connected with God is to become like God." Then surely we all want faith, and it is worth every effort requisite to obtain it.

Faith is the assent to a proposition that seems reasonable. Reasoning proceeds from parts to a whole or from the whole to parts.

Then if the propositions we have learned thus far sound reasonable, if we assent to them we certainly have faith in the rules and the necessity for using them.

Not the belief that they are all very well for some one else. That is not faith. But such a belief in them that we cling to them with patient persistence to overcome mortal beliefs, with steadfast endurance of all scorn and ridicule; all opposition.

Some people here these statements, see the reason in them and set out to use them. They do well for awhile and are filled with delight at the Law.

But as they have not rid themselves of all the old ways of thinking, and still allow themselves to talk with those who do according to mortal ways, sickness comes upon them.

They are afraid Spirit will not save them and forsake it, or they listen to the advice of others and try something else in its place or with it, or they conclude that it is a beautiful religion but not a thorough healing Principle, or they think they are not proficient enough in its use to risk it alone.

This is the time to prove the faith that they thought they possessed. Faith stands firm in the midst of trial or temptation of all kinds.

In creation the fourth step was, "And God said, Let there be a firmament in the midst of the waters." Firmament means fixed foundation-definite expanse.

We said in the first lesson that Spirit moving upon the face of the waters, meant the word of Truth-or God-acting upon the mind, thus the fourth step is, Let there be a fixed foundation in the midst of mind-a well established basis that nothing can shake. Let it separate the conscious thoughts of truth from conscious thoughts of error. We must have a fixed or firm mind. If we have this firm mind we shall have no sickness or trouble, for they are but the results of wrong thoughts, of a wavering, uncertain state of mind. "Unstable as water and thou shalt not excel."

Water is ever changing, and there must be a firmament in the midst to separate that which is under from that which is above. The thoughts that are under or below are untrue, those that are above are true. The untrue are doubt, fear, discouragement, uncertainty, and they bring sickness and trouble.

The true thoughts are, that God is in every place, fills all space in the universe. That God is Spirit, and that this Spirit is the only thing that is substantial, upon which we can lean or rely; therefore is substance.

That this Spirit is Health itself, Strength itself, Life itself, Love itself, Truth itself, Happiness itself. That in this Spirit we each live and move and have our being, are of it, created by and of it, and cannot be separated from it.

If we stop to consider these words we cannot help seeing that we are therefore inseparable from perfect Life, Health, Truth, Love, Strength, and Happiness. They fill space, so we cannot get outside of them. When we have our mind *fixed* upon these foundation statements of Truth so firmly that nothing can turn us, nothing shake us, we have faith: the faith that connects us with God and makes us like God, or rather proves how like Him we are in reality.

We must speak the true words until our faith is established. Right thinking and right speaking bring faith. At first, when we speak true words and they bring good and quick results, it is not because we have faith in the doctrine itself so much as in the instructions we have received; faith that if we do certain things the result will be as we have been told: that is, we really have faith in the word of the one who taught us, faith in his experience.

This is better than no faith at all; but when it is tested, we find what it is worth. It is easily shaken and disturbed, because it depends upon the knowledge of another, which has been reflected upon us.

We watch anxiously for results of our words, and when we do not see any we are discouraged, disheartened and doubting, sometimes even doubting the Law itself. The fault is in ourselves, for while we look for the results we have no faith. It is doubt our fear or failure that makes us watch. Fear is always doubt in whatever form it shows itself.

Real faith rests in the Lord. He does the work. We only speak the word that He takes care of, and we, having performed our part, must leave the rest to Him, taking no thought for the morrow.

There is no time with God, for "a thousand years are as a day" with Him. All is now; we have nothing to do with any future. Our sole work is to "do the duty that lies nearest thee" each moment, and God, who created and sustains us, will see to results. The firm mind that has true faith is fixed upon the well established basis of the law and has supreme trust in God, with perfect patience and the peace that is born of understanding that however evil things may seem they are not so in reality.

We can easily test our faith and know whether it is genuine, or whether it is simply hope.

If we have trouble do we say it is a delusion and a falsity for only Good can come to us, or do we cry and mourn just like other people who never heard of the Law of Spirit?

It is very easy to believe in wrong and to believe what the senses perceive, but while we do we are looking at shadows cast by images. Images formed by our own thoughts.

We must have the firm mind that shall divide the waters of our thoughts, sending the false ones to right and to left; relegate them to oblivion where they belong, and keep only true thoughts.

We must close the senses for they do not tell the truth. There is no other way to get faith but to tell the truth about things and stop talking falsely.

While we tell that a man has rheumatism we speak falsely, for God made man perfect and in His own likeness.

Can God have sickness of any kind? No. Then it is not true that his image has it either, or can be sick at all.

We have principle to declare over and over before we can prove it. We must speak the words of truth with confidence in their efficacy. Say strongly, firmly, I know that only the Good is true and powerful; that only good reigns and that evil is but seeming. There is no evil upon the earth. God is my refuge, my strength, and I am not afraid of anything at all. God is all. There is nothing else.-

These words are our salvation and will make us firm and clear for God has promised, "To him that ordereth his conversation aright will I show the salvation of God." Hundreds can testify that the promise is true.

If we have faith in our principle the words will work with us, for us and through us. Thus our use of them is a test of our faith, for the whole world is against them, has no belief in them, but if we have true faith we care nothing for aught but truth, no matter who opposes.

People often criticize this doctrine and say that Christ did not teach this in order. How does any one know in what order he taught?

According to Gospel history He seems to have taught as occasion presented itself. He gave them precepts to live by, not metaphysical studies. He taught principally by symbolism or parable, and even the disciples did not always comprehend his meaning.

As the four accounts of his life differ in some respects, how can we tell anything about his order of procedure?

Three of them concur in saying that Jesus retired to a solitary mountain, where he had some spiritual experience and from whence he came forth with power. One says, "Jesus returned in the power of the Spirit." Two agree that his teaching began by saying, " The Kingdom of God is at hand; repent ye," or turn to it.

The disciple who loved him and whom he loved, and who would for that reason be more apt to remember his wordsgives the first ones to be "Follow me," and the next teaching "Except a man be born again he cannot see the Kingdom of God," indicating some change.

Jesus taught them that this change was a mental one because he said it was of Spirit and compared it to the silence of the wind.

There is no one of the gospels so full of love as the book of John, and it is full of teaching that calls God Father and of the love He bears men. In this account, Jesus teaches that God is Spirit and tells men to search the Scriptures. He said, "He that heareth my word and believeth on God hath everlasting life."

All the gospels teach that God is all, does all, and that He is Good; that denial of mortal (fleshly) self is the way to follow His will; that to pray for whatever we desire is simply to have faith that God does grant all desires, and that we shall receive what we wish.

These are the three propositions of Spiritual Law. All the teachings of this law are from the life and words of Christ and explain His words according to a scientific understanding of Spiritual Law, or the only true law. The law of God is the only law.

It is Jesus Christ and Him only that all are to follow, imitate, and learn of. He said, "follow *me*."

It seems as if this was the age of criticism. We wonder that critics who pride themselves upon their ability to find flaws in everything, have never stopped to think that criticism is weakness instead of power. Love is power, and "love taketh not account of evil but rejoiceth with the truth."

If we rejoice in the Truth we have no time nor disposition to look for errors anywhere. And we certainly have not understanding of Spirit grafted into our lives if we criticize any one at all.

The only perfect teacher of Truth is he or she who teaches the charity that is love; love so broad that it embraces all people, all theories, all doctrines, seeing good in all and ignoring anything except good. Not one word of weak criticism, not one word of doubtful praise, not one word of disapproval of anyone or anything. The law of Spirit of Love.

Out of all the teachers or men who have appeared in the world, only one taught absolute truth with no admixture of error.

Many have taught beautiful and lofty truths, but with those truths were mingled errors and mistakes. Abraham taught polygamy, David warfare, Paul, the subjection of woman. Solomon taught slavery.

But Jesus, the one perfect teacher taught freedom from bondage; love and tenderness to all; charity for all, even for the sinner. He taught the equality of man and woman and the respect due to woman, for he honored his mother.

Then He is the one perfect teacher and the one we are to follow. It is the words that he spoke, that we speak with such wonderful results—words of truth.

And whoever has spoken them in the past even though he did not quite understand their power, has shown forth their potency in a great measure.

Daniel, had no fear of lions. Men passed through fire unharmed and had heavy vehicles passed over their bodies without feeling them. The reason no one proved the whole power of words of truth was because all were so afraid of death, and their fear came upon them. Jesus "came to deliver those who through this fear of death were all their lifetime subject to bondage."

We have the same true words and whenever we speak them our mind acts in a certain way. All minds act alike only some understand more quickly than others.

All experience of the mind is in the way to show forth spiritual understanding which is the goal to which we all hasten.

This spiritual understanding is not a power of the intellect. It is not a mortal comprehension at all. It cannot come until the mind springs beyond the bounds of mortal understanding. It is the divine spark within us meeting and recognizing the Truth of God.

It is immortal understanding. When we have this understanding of Truth we cannot be sick or poor or unhappy or in doubt or fear, for we have true faith.

Fear is but doubt of what is true for if we believe wholly in Truth we cannot fear, there is no room for fear.

Jesus taught that Spirit is the only Presence, the only Power and the only Wisdom. Have we faith in this Truth?

If so we shall go on in the true understanding until we know that we also are one with the Spirit of Power and Wisdom. "One is your father even God." "God is Spirit." Spirit is the Father of us all and we are "of one substance with the Father."

When we have true faith we shall be "wise unto salvation" and have the power to lift others out of seeming darkness, for in the Only Presence, all are one. We shall know for ourselves that "flesh profiteth nothing," for words of Truth only are Spirit and are Life, and we shall realize all the promises of God to all who seek and find him.

"When thou walkest through the waters I will be with thee and through the rivers they shall not overflow." The almighty shall be thy defense and thou shalt have plenty of silver." "The flames shall not devour thee. Thou shalt be hid from the scourge of the tongue. At destruction and famine thou shalt laugh. Thou shalt be safe from the arrow that flieth by day and the pestilence that walketh at midnight."

Thus we see that no good thing is withheld from those who are Spiritually minded and from all called evil they are protected.

We can say to all seeming evil and sickness with our spiritual understanding. "Peace, be still."

Let us strive for the faith in its highest is understanding. When trial comes, seeming to overflow, let is rise and say, *I know that none of this is* true, *for God is working through me and for me and by me.* And stand there as immovable as "the everlasting hills."

This is faith, and when the test comes to prove whether we have it, let us be firm, be steadfast, for if we stand the test, if our faith is sure, we are in the way of spiritual understanding.

# NOTES

NOTES

# CHAPTER V.

## Nature and Office of Mind Work.

We have now come to the fifth orderly step in our study of Mind. After faith come works for, "Faith if it have not works is dead in itself." We must now show by what we do, prove, whether we have true faith or not, and of what quality it is.

Paul said, "If I have all faith so as to remove mountains, but have not love, I am nothing." So another test of our faith is whether we are ready to use the power we believe in for others as well as use it constantly for ourselves. We have learned that all are one, then all who know not this beautiful Law are in our care. We *are* our brothers' keepers. We have work to do without, as well as within our own minds.

The fifth step in creation was, "Let the waters under the heavens be gathered together unto one place, and let the dry land appear." "Under the heavens" must be on the earth, and as "waters" means thoughts, mind must gather its thoughts together so they will be fixed, just as dry land is more fixed than water. Water is ever restless, unsettled, and changing, and so are mortal thoughts.

The mind forms a firm foundation or faith, by its conscious choice of Truth, and the next step is to determine to hold to this Truth at whatever cost to mortal ways of thinking. This is the dry land of the mind brought out by effort.

It takes self-training to exchange old conditions, old ways of thinking for new ones. Paul said, "Work out your own salvation" and that is just what we must do, each and every one of us. It requires constant effort on our part and no one can do it for us.

The Law of Spirit is not a mere theory or simply a beautiful religious belief. It is religion itself, that permeates the whole being and renovates every thought. It is truly a re-binding of the soul to God.

When grain its threshed the weeds that have grown up with it are separated from it blown away, leaving nothing but pure grain to pass through the machine. The weeds are light while the grain is heavy enough not to be blown out.

Our mortal (human) thoughts are light and easily blown about by every wind of doctrine. We must blow them away by denial and have only true thoughts that are firm and unchangeable. They are of God and from God, and we thus re-bind them to God; fix them upon the basis where they belong.

When Adam left his high estate by listening to his own sensuous thought (serpent) the Law told him that he should "till the ground" from thenceforth.

To till is to plow and prepare for seed. Thus we find *our* work. We must prepare the soil of our mind for the seed of Truth, by using the rules of right reasoning, or tilling the earth.

When the earth is plowed all rubbish is cast out and thrown far from the soil to be cultivated. This is the kind of work we have to do first of all. Watch our thoughts and cast out the wrong ones by denial that the seeds of truth may grow umimpeded.

It was further said that man must "bruise the head" of sense thoughts (the serpent) for they "bruise the heel" of man.

our thoughts are indeed sorely bruised by living in the senses and that is what brings sickness, pain and trouble. The senses bruise the body (heel) of man.

We must take these sense thoughts by the head and bruise them; cut them off by denial, working patiently and persistently as the farmer works in tilling his ground. Man was given "dominion over all the earth" by his Maker and it is our duty, our work, to subdue the earth mind.

In order to understand this work that we are to do we must study our own mind that we may know how it works. There is in man a principle or faculty, which seems to lie dormant so surrounded is it by the darkness of mortal ways of thought. It is the "light that lighteth every man that cometh into the world" and is truly "hid under a bushel" in the form of false ideas.

"The light shineth in the darkness and the darkness apprehendeth it not." We must remove the darkness by bringing forth the light, for what we call darkness is but the light hidden.

The command was, "Le there be light," and this is our work with self if we would be re-bound to the Creator. Our work is that of recreating or regenerating, which is being born again. This light then that is within each of us must be understood and brought out.

It has had various names, for all people of the earth have known of its existence. Some have called it the "still small voice," some the "daemon," others "conscience," and again others have said it was the "God within."

But by whatever name it was called, all history agrees

that whoever listened to and obeyed its promptings had satisfaction, even when they did not fully comprehend its nature.

Job spoke of it as "a spirit in man and the inspiration of the Almighty giveth them understanding." He was quite right for if this inward monitor is listened to it bringeth understanding, which is the acme of satisfaction or the highest good, for which all have sought, both ancient and modern.

This is not intellect for it is beyond above it in power and comprehension. It is intuition of the Spirit, or the intuitive faculty. It is the highest of man-the real-man true self which must come forth, be born again, for it was created in us, or rather is the only real creation. We must break the burr that seems to encase intuition; burst our bonds and be free.

How shall we gain freedom? It is very easy if we only persist. It is only to speak words. "Let us take with us words and return unto our God." They must be holy, true words, or words of truth about God and self, and all creation.

So much has been made of intellect all over the world, all through the ages that we do not like to be told that is nothing worth. That seems like blasphemy to the proud mortal mind.

Whoever cultivates the true mind, the spirit, knows how much greater are its powers than those of intellect. There has been altogether too much religion of the intellect, a trying to rebind the intellect to the Infinite Mind, which can never be done, and which resulted in contempt of all who did not agree as to the correct binding process. Not only contempt but persecution.

The work we are to do is not that kind at all. It is wholly a work of love for which we must train our own mind. What has the intellect with all its boasted power ever brought to man?

Has it brought happiness or health? Has it made him love his neighbor as himself, thus fulfilling the law of God?

On the contrary it has made him hard, cold and selfish, and has hastened him on the grave through pain and suffering without confidence in man or God. Job said, "There is a way that seemeth right unto a man but the end thereof are ways of death." Such a way is the way of intellect and all the way of mortal thought.

But there is a way to gain knowledge aside from the intellect, and we may know all that has ever been known all that books have contained if we never see a library. Every man has access to the Infinite Mind wherein is all knowledge. Emerson, in speaking of this said, "What Plato has thought, man may think; what a saint has felt, he may feel."

Until we understand this it seems very strange to us that each time we have an entirely new thought-as we suppose, something quite original-behold, the very next book we look into has that very idea expressed, and was very likely written five hundred or two thousand or more years ago. Then we conclude that we are no different from others, and that Solomon was right in saying, "There is nothing new under the sun."

But understanding of Spirit explains all this for the voice of truth in the soul is one, and all who listen will speak the same language. It is a fact that all who speak truth say the same things, even the same words, very often.

Jesus Christ needed no teacher but his Father, and we need no other. We have the same Father. Jesus taught a way to think that would bring life, health and strength to the body, and judgment and wisdom to the mind.

We have no desire to depreciate the knowledge obtained from books for it is of the greatest value in associating with our fellow men. It makes men acquainted with each other and the world. We only mean to emphasize the truth that there is even a higher knowledge, and often the most "learned" lack this vital wisdom. It is a deplorable fact that the "man of letters" is not always a good man. And often the poor man living in his hut shows that he lives and walks with God.

Jesus taught that we should have anything we desire if we only believe that God will give it; if we only have true faith or trust. There is no one so strong, peaceful and powerful as the one who trusts with a real genuine confidence in God. Trust will bring to pass all we desire.

Jesus taught to pray, and to pray as if we had already received the desired blessing. Prayer is affirmation as our third lesson explained. The prayer of the mind is the word or declaration of the mind.

Whatever we declare we are sure to have, for God has created all things good, and for us, and it is our office to speak the word that will make them show forth. All round about us in an invisible power (invisible to the senses) that our word acts upon, bringing it into action. Whatever we desire can be invoked into sight. We have just what we invoke. If we continually speak of hateful things they will surround us. We can speak into visibility exactly what we wish.

All things in what we call nature are in abeyance, are invisible until some force of mind calls them out.

And thus all things we can desire are in the silence and invisibility until the force of a true word brings them forth. Words are magnets and draw whatever is like unto them; of the same nature. They are like flint and tinder being struck together to produce flame, for they strike that in invisibility which springs into action like fire.

If we speak with faith we *shall* receive. "A man shall be satisfied with good by the fruit of this mouth," said Job.

Words are far more potent than we ever dreamed before we studied mind and its mysterious and wonderful ways of procedure, and we must be very careful to use only good, true words, for "according to thy faith be it unto thee," is Law.

If we believe in evil we are having faith in evil and it will be so unto us. We have learned that evil is not real, and we have learned to reject it. Then we must abide by our rules and declare only good.

If we would only cling to the true thoughts that belong to the real of us, the divine self or "God within," listen only to this "still small voice," we should not need to puzzle ourselves about conscious and unconscious, mortal and immortal mind, as metaphysicians call it.

But as we seem more inclined to pursue the thoughts that lead to an end and show out as pain and trouble, we must try to understand these distinctions.

The ways of thinking that are always veering about in

uncertain manner are called mortal because they are none of them true and lasting but belong to "flesh that profiteth nothing," or as Paul expressed it to the natural (mortal) body. This mortal body is always changing as the thoughts of mortal mind change, for these bodily conditions are but the pictures of thoughts.

The body is like the screen upon which pictures are thrown from a camera, and mortal mind is the camera that receives the images, or thoughts. For instance, a thought is impressed upon or received into mortal mind and its image is thrown by the convex glass of mortal mind on to the surface called body and shows the picture we call a tumor, or rheumatism, or any other condition. The picture of everything we see is impressed upon the retina of the eye and remains there for some time. If we see disagreeable objects the images are the same. The body is like the retina of the eye and produces just what our thoughts rest upon.

Then we must take care what images are received by our mortal mind and have them only true and spiritual, if we would have a strong, healthy, perfect body. We know that as quickly as we can think if anything an image of that thought is instantly before us mentally. That image is as quickly transferred to the body or reflected by it; pictured upon it.

Now in reality or in the realm of realities (which is Spirit) there is but One Mind and it thinks only true thoughts.

Then the thoughts of evil are from no mind at all for such a mind is as unreal as the evil it tries to believe in. We speak of this mind as if it had existence, in order to explain these conditions that seem so real to people who do not know truth.

It has been called mortal mind because all its ways are Mortal or fleshly, material ones. Mortal thinking is not really a power at all, but is a misuse of power. It is like chasing a shadow.

We become like what we study or associate with, always. If we should continually study shadows should we not become nonentities like the shadows?

That is just what we do if we study mortal ways, for mortal is nothing whatever whether we apply it to the body or mind. If we study, talk and think of matter, or mortal thoughts, we become nothing, or unreal, untrue and substanceless.

God is the only Substance there is in the universe; and God is Spirit. Then Spirit is all there is anywhere, and whatever is not of Spirit is nowhere, has no real existence, is but a figment of what is but a false claim to be something. A false way of thinking trying to establish is ways as true. It is as if a shadow tried to prove itself something substantial.

The mortal or fleshly body which is made by what we call mortal thoughts, or the fluctuating, vacillating, untrue thoughts, is as a shadow compared to the real true body which is spiritual, being formed by spiritual thoughts.

The mind that thinks true thoughts is immortal Mind. It speaks true works for it declares itself as all, and flesh and material things to be nothing.

Whoever speaks true words speaks them with the true immortal mind of him and will see all things become as new. Pain and disease go away. Things of matter lose their hold. Evil has no power. The body changes for it loses its earthiness, and the face is radiant with the light of Spirit. The divine self is showing forth, and will do so more and more unto the perfect day when it is indeed all Spirit, if true words are persistently spoken.

Truth is the Christ and when we speak true words Christ comes to us and takes up his abode in us together with the Father, so that we have life eternal right here and now.

It is for us to make our choice which we will believe, the true or the false. To refuse to believe in the false is to repent, to turn to the true. To deny the false is to wash away sins, for sin is mistake or error. Forgiveness is the giving of truth in place of error.

To have sins washed away by the blood of Christ is to have errors made nothing by the word of Truth, for Christ means Truth, and blood means word. Blood is supposed to be life, and "my words are life," said Christ.

To keep the true words in mind is to make the body strong and well, for the body always shows exactly the way we have thought.

Our present thoughts are our conscious thoughts, while those that are past are unconscious thoughts that have formed the body. If we wish strong, healthy bodies we must have right true thoughts. We can make our bodies what we please.

If we indulge in a fit of anger we may expect our blood to be thin and watery.

If we think we are wicked and sinful we may become invalids. If we hold false thoughts we shall have miserable bodies, and not only that but all near us are affected by our thoughts.

It is hard at first to deny the evidence of the senses, but if we persevere after awhile we see and know the true way and we are joyous and glad.

When we first accept the Truth it is by intellectual assent. It seems reasonable to the intellect. But after a while we begin to doubt one statement or another as we meet some sorrow or sin or pain which is not at once overcome.

We had supposed that the rules would accomplish everything and that we were out of danger if all such things; that the word spoken was to turn everything right about.

But had we real faith as we spoke the word, or was it a trembling hope that we entertained, that the words would work, or was it that we wished to test the power of the Law of Truth?

It was not true genuine faith that he had, or the words would have proved effective. For a word of truth is quick and powerful to save from everything, if we have faith in it. Of course anything spoke coldly and heartlessly, or carelessly, is inefficient.

No matter who speaks truth in earnest, or where it is found or how clumsily told, when the whole truth is told, people must be saved.

Doubt is a stumbling block to ourselves, but if we speak true words over and over even before we quite believe in their power, or quite understand them, they will bear fruit, for they will reach someone else who is ready for them, and take effect in their minds.

No word of truth is ever lost. If we keep speaking words

of truth they will at length take hold of our own mind and bring faith.

There is no work we cannot do believing in truth, for it is a silent Principle full of power. The working of truth or spiritual law is as silent process, and we speak the words in the silence. When we have done so until our own mind is set into the way of right thinking we are a power to all about us and the word we speak will heal our neighbor either in body or mind.

We shall if we go on with our silent work of self-training become so invested with power that our presence will heal without any effort of ours. We become so at one with the truth we have spoken over and over till we love it, that our knowing it, our certainty of it fills us with a vital potency that emanates or radiates from us and lifts all who come near us from their state of materiality, whether it is pain, sorrow or sin.

We are each a living witness to the efficiency of truth, and a silent protest against error, and all who have errors (sins) must drop them or be made to suffer, for our mental and spiritual attitude carries a powerful conviction of the justice and expediency of the moral law-the law of God-and all who do not wish to abide by it cannot endure our presence. Often they are made sick by their opposition to the truth we express.

All who are willing to see the purity and beauty of truth are turned; thus providing that, "The law of the Lord is perfect, converting the soul."

If we did not see the fruits of our speaking we must keep on, never relaxing our efforts, for "Patience worketh experience," and experience makes both faith and trust. We must never think of speak of failure. There is no such thing in the kingdom of God where we are working. There is nothing but success, and we must talk always on the side of success.

The word of Truth is the Spirit of Truth and it is ever present and will lead us into the understanding of all truth where we cannot get mixed up with false doctrines.

We can prove our doctrine whether it be of God or of man, for "By their fruits ye shall know them."

Jesus said, "These signs shall follow them that believe; in my name they shall cast out devils; they shall speak new tongues; they shall lay lands on the sick and they shall recover."

All who truly have faith in this doctrine and live and work accordingly, do have these signs follow. Is that not proof that it is the doctrine of Christ?

Some people who have depended upon the Jesus of theology feel as if this doctrine took him away from them because it says that it is the word of Truth spoken that saves from evil. They are still clinging to the man of flesh just as the disciples clung to him.

Instead of taking away Jesus the Christ it brings him nearer because we understand how to get near to him. He is always near us. "I am with you always" were his very words. He is the very example of the word of truth spoken-the perfect living witness to its power. He came to bear witness to the Truth of the word of Truth, and therefore was called the Christ, for Christ means Truth.

Truth is God, then Christ was (and is) God. This does not differ from any theology ever taught. But it does not mean as people have seemed to think, that the manifest flesh of Jesus was God-the flesh that could be looked upon with physical eyes; for, "No man (of flesh) hath seen God at any time," said John.

Jesus Christ was the manifestation of the word of Truth. He was that word. If we cling close to the word of Truth how can He be taken away from us? We are one with Him in God. He was and is Spirit and we are that same Spirit.

His words were, "I in them and thou in me." Then we are all one, and each must learn to say and realize as He did, "I and my father are one." Then we shall bring forth the works that he did knowing that God alone doeth the works. "God works through you to will and to do."

God lives through us the Life that is eternal. God thinks through us the eternal perfect thought. We have our being in the Mind that is God.

There are people who fear the science of Spirit because it takes away their belief in a material heaven. This has never been the teaching of the Bible or the church. The Bible says plainly, "Flesh and blood cannot inherit the kingdom of heaven." How closely people must be wedded to a material, fleshly life to desire a material heaven.

Can there be anyone who does not know from experience that the highest, deepest pleasure is mental; that no material pleasure is lasting; that luxury if flesh is not real joy? Is there one who will say that pain of body is at all equal to pain of mind? Is there one who would choose material luxury before peace of mind? A palace with a troubled heart, mind or conscience? If there is such a one to be found of course he could not understand the satisfaction of harmony. Heaven is harmony, and if it is not attainable here it will never be found anywhere.

As there is no such thing as real happiness connected with material things, there can be no such thing as a material heaven. Happiness is of mind-Spirit. Heaven is a purely spiritual state, but it changes all things to and for us, even material things.

When we find this state we also find that we have power over all things below Spirit, because Spirit is the only power there is. It has complete sway and all else must stand aside.

The real man-the creation of God-was created to "have dominion over all the earth." This includes flesh, for flesh is considered "of the earth, earthy."

This is the birthright of man as has been well expressed:

> "O God! I am one forever
> With thee, by the glory of birth,
> Thy celestial powers proclaim it,
> To the uttermost bounds of earth."

# NOTES

# NOTES

### Spiritual Understanding.

The sixth in the study of mind is spiritual understanding. It is spiritual knowledge, or the wisdom spoken of by seers and prophets of old. It is the highest shining forth of mind, or the realization of truth itself, and is the goal toward which all study, all work, all faith points.

It is the fullness of the bread of eternal life, which supplies man with the nutriment for a perfect character. It is the elixir of life, so long sought in vain. Alchemists of old plead for victims to their insatiable demand for human blood, as well as for gold, with which to supply their fruitless endeavors to prepare an elixir of perennial youth.

The true elixir was given by Jesus nineteen hundred years ago, and was unheeded, but now after all these darkened, blinded ages, we return to His words, that when understood bring the spiritual understanding that constitutes eternal life.

We have learned that in order to obtain the highest knowledge of mind, we must reject or deny all beliefs that oppose the statements concerning universal good. The chapter upon denial taught us this, and the one upon affirmation teaches what we are to declare in order to be 'clothed and in our right mind," or in order to have our thoughts right, that the body may be well.

Then we were taught that faith is the next step on the way to understanding, and that "faith without works is dead," therefore we must work faithfully to obtain the understanding that makes all work our highest joy, and what is greatness of faith- a sure knowledge of all that truth is, and will do.

Knowledge of Good brings understanding, if we live in accordance with the precepts of the good or according to the law. We have been told that "Love is the fulfilling of the law." Then it is love that we are to live in accord with. We are to show forth love; the love that thinketh no evil whatever, no matter what the appearance is. For spiritual understanding is love itself, and inasmuch as we show forth true love, we prove how far on toward full understanding we are, for, "by their fruits ye shall know them."

People have always watched the works of others to see if their professions bore fruits, and they always will watch. There is nothing so easily discerned as the fruit of understanding, for one who has it is of the same "mind which was in Christ Jesus" and does the like work-is of one mind with God, or, rather, proves his unity with God.

The work that proceeds from understanding is unmistakable, for as Daniel said, "The people that do know their God shall be strong and do exploits," and to have spiritual understanding is to know God intimately.

We can learn much from the ancients, even from those we call heathen. The portion of Hindu literature that specially treats of a Supreme Being, is named Unpanishad. The original meaning of the word was "to sit near a teacher and submissively listen to him," and the latest meaning is "truth, or divine revelation." This shows how they were in the habit of gaining their highest knowledge. It is the same submissive listening, that we are to cultivate in order to attain understanding. Our teacher is God, for "it is God who giveth understanding," said the man noted for wisdom. He must have known whereof he spoke.

We must not mistake the feeling that we have when we read some truth that impresses us deeply, for spiritual understanding. Reading something that finds a response in our mind, that wakes an echo in our being with a flash of conviction that it is true, is simply a chord that has vibrated to the touch of another mind, and not genuine understanding till we live the doctrine to which we so respond.

The real understanding-or realization of truth-proves its genuineness at once, for it demonstrates its reality by showing its mastery through us over all our mortal conditions-sin, sickness, death, trouble, poverty, and all that we call undesirable.

Understanding is power to do all the works belonging to mind; healing, converting, quickening, cleansing of the world around us. One who has understanding proves by his works that he knows God, has been with Him, has listened to His voice, because He heals all who need healing by the word of His speaking. He uplifts all who come into His presence and purifies the very atmosphere.

All work is the same whether we heal or teach, write, or just send our thoughts broadcast over the waiting world. Healing is teaching, for it is simply telling the truth over and over to the patient; teaching is healing, for the truth always heals; writing not only tells the truth, but carries the healing power in every word; thinking truly both teaches and heals the world.

We are all endowed with this understanding, for the love

that constitutes it gave us and still gives us life. But are we in different degrees of progress toward showing it forth.

This is what makes a seeming difference in people who study Mind-or God- and those who are just beginning are not always able to comprehend all that the advanced students say and do, anymore than a little child learning his alphabet can understand the equation of payments. This is the cause of the misunderstanding among students of the same subjects; but understanding of the Law emphatically teaches to judge not. It teaches the broadest charity for all, even for those still in ignorance, and as Paul said, "especially for those of the household of faith."

Nothing will hasten us into the shining forth of understanding more surely than doing kindly and speaking kindly to all who are trying to help the world by healing and teaching with the truth, even if they have not the same interpretation of it in every particular that we have. "There are diversities of gifts, but the same spirit." They use all the light they have.

If we speak unkindly of our neighbor's character or work, or of his ministry of healing and teaching, we have not the love that is understanding, for those who have it have no desire to speak unjustly or unkindly of anyone. They fellowship with all the world in love and nothing can resist love. It is powerful and fearless. God is love.

If we knew anything of the law of Spirit, self-preservation alone would keep us from speaking critically of one who is doing his or her best, for to do so is only throwing a shadow over our own powers and will not harm the one we criticize, for "they shall be hid from scourge of the tongue."

If we hold prejudice we carry about with us a dark shadow that will hinder our own work. Criticism and rebuke are to the mind as acid to the blood, and impede the light of our understanding.

We must cleanse the thought of uncharitableness by denial, as one cleanses the blood from acid. We give nourishing food to purify the blood, and in like manner, we must give the mind the pure food of true thoughts, of loving kind thoughts, that there may be no room for uncharitable ones.

Charity is the most rapidly working and powerful feeling of the mind, for it is love at work, and makes us love all mankind justly and generously. It eases and heals us, binds us to all mankind and causes us to shine with understanding.

We must refuse to criticize the beliefs of people-their creeds-for these creeds have given great help to those who had no other light.

We must not say that the orderly arrangement of mental processes is not scientific, for we hereby show ignorance of mind.

If we say that "mental" is a wrong term to apply to the science of Spirit, we show that we do not remember that Mind is Spirit. The science of Mind is surely mental science.

To say that "spiritual" is a better term than "mental" shows that we have caught the meaning of but one word instead of two words. Spirit and Mind are identical terms in truth.

Some do not like one term and some another, but this is foolishness. All words are wide and deep and lofty when they are names of deity. We must not stop criticize names, but give them the noblest significance possible, for to understand grandly and nobly will make us grand and noble in our work.

Our work is to cause the light to shine in dark places by causing sickness, feebleness and age to drop away from men, and true health to spring forth, and sorrow, sin and death to flee before the joy, peace and life we call forth by our words, for we only prove to the world the perfect estate of goodness whereunto all were created.

Our work is to speak the truth to our neighbor, and that truth is plainly given. It is not calling each other poor worms of the dust, or unscientific cheats, or anything that no child of God ever was, since God made them in His own image and likeness.

In speaking to our neighbor we have a powerful but dangerous instrument at our command. By speaking only truth we use it for our own and others' blessedness. By speaking falsehood we hide ourselves from peace and happiness, for every word we speak goes forth only to come back with double the power with which we sent it forth. A true word is twice blessed: it blesses him who gives and him who receives, and more, for it returns to the giver with an added blessing.

This instrument of health and disease is the tongue. A great deal has been said of it by scripture writers. James calls it "a little member, but a fire and world of iniquity: an unruly evil full of poison," and says no man can tame it. He was speaking of mortal man and was quite right, for mortal man never has tamed the tongue. It has been and is a source of evil themselves" as David predicted. Solomon said, "Death and life are in the power of the tongue."

We have been taught that from certain fetid localities arises miasma that creates pestilence. Is there anything more foul and deadly than a slanderous uncharitable tongue, and is it not the miasma from such in the aggregate that produces what is called pestilence?

In a recently preached sermon, Talmage said that "God put His finger upon Vesuvius and destroyed Pompeii and Herculanem, as He destroyed Sodom, Gomorahh, and three other ancient cities, all for profligacy, and that He has plenty more volcanic monsters to let loose upon our modern wicked cities."

His God then, is a destructive force, through fear of whom people must be controlled. This is the idea of God that has reigned for so many ages; but fear of Him has never made people happy and good. It has only made persecution and bloodshed rife in His name. Under the name of worship of this God every crime has been committed against His creations.

Our God is not of this kind and never destroys, for He is only good, and Good is the only Creator.

The destructive force is thoughts of sense. Were not all those cities given over entirely to sense life and thought? Can we suppose that there was a single truly spiritual minded inhabitant? For even their gods were sense gods. Did not their own impure thoughts filling the atmosphere cause their destruction?

Material science teaches that impurities will cause spontaneous combustion, as do certain gases in the atmosphere when united.

According to the science of Mind impure thoughts vitiate the atmosphere and are veritable nitroglycerine, bringing volcanoes to action. Error is its own destruction.

What need there is that the world be taught the importance of thought, and that they are thus responsible for their own lives instead of being taught to fear the only power there is, and which is only good; instead of being taught that God is the cause of destruction.

So the first step toward the understanding of truth is to guard each thought and word and keep them true, for words of truth spoken either audibly or silently, heal and make wise and peaceful. They quicken to action such a change for the better that we wonder how so great a power has been unobserved for so long.

We no longer worry over things that once troubled us, for we know how to put that all from us by the word of our speaking.

True words cause us to enter into a new country where disease, sin and death are not known. All is health and joy, peace and plenty, home and harmony. These things are ours, for "by our words we are justified." We become just like our words.

True words open the very portals of Heaven and disclose to our view and for our possession, all its glorious blessings, because true words bring harmony within and around us, and harmony is Heaven. It is easy to see that if we are in a state of harmony, all who come near us are influenced by it.

We have all seen the effect one cheerful person has upon a room full of people who are disposed to be rather gloomy. It is like a stream of sunshine in a dark room. And we have also seen one gloomy countenance throw a shadow over a number of people and cause a feeling of depression.

These states of mind are quickly transmitted and they are illustrations of the power of thought being transferred from one to another. How one malicious, revengeful person can affect others by talking, carrying the venom of his disposition in his words and manner even to the extent of making them ill, so potent is this mental influence. If these are the effects of the untrue condition of thought and word, how powerful the true word must be, and *is*.

True words teach us of our wisdom as Spirit-one with all wisdom-for understanding is wisdom from on high, shining upon us and through us and from us, without measure.

True words disclose to us that we are one with all power for they heal and bless as has been declared, "the tongue of the wise is health."

To speak truth is to shine with spirituality, to glow with power, to be clear of perception, and to show forth the glory of understanding, for "the entrance of thy words giveth light." To speak truth is to be God-like.

This wisdom from on high, or understanding, does not come from reading of books, giving of lectures, talking in a scientific manner or memorizing statements to repeat to others. If we would understand the doctrine we must do the will.

Talking ever so fluently is not doing the will, although it may give to someone else the truth to live by. Talking truth one moment and talking condemnation of someone whose ways differ from ours, or who does not act as we think is proper, the next moment, is not speaking truth; is not living it, "by our words we are condemned."

Sometimes people erroneously think that they can use this law to decree against others. They do not consider their words, for they mean that they will use God to destroy His own children. Those are not true words for the moment any one speaks such he has descended into mortal mind; he has not spoken at all; he is worse than dumb for he has tried to pervert truth itself. This is far from "the mind that was in Christ Jesus "and is an unknown language in the new country-the country of Spirit.

This is not wisdom, for, "The wisdom that is from above is first pure, then peaceable, gentle, and easy to be entreated, full or mercy and good fruits."

While true understanding brings power it brings humility. There is no feeling of mastery one over another, only over error. True words are all of love, and if I speak any other words I do not speak at all, for they are not the utterance of truth. We do not speak true words until the mortal is put quite away-hushed.

It would be a terrible thing for mortal man to be invested with infinite power and would soon bring chaos. If one thought of mortal self intrudes we have left our high estate, lost our power, are not truly alive, nay worse than dead for we have betrayed our trust, sold our birthright and forfeited our places as workers for and in God. It is not God that works through us then.

If we indulge one wish toward anyone, that is not kind and loving or that would cause him pain or suffering even if deserved, we are from understanding, far from the country where we long to be. The law of this new country is inexorable and takes care of each inhabitant. If we break one jot or title of this law, we suffer and no one need wish to hasten the suffering. It is sure to come; we are perfectly sure to reap as we have sown and it is better to keep each thought of our own clear, pure, and kind, so that we have none to come back like a poisoned dart.

We must use the rules for setting aside our own false ways, that our spiritual nature may shine forth, and let our neighbor alone if we cannot silently deny error and declare him good.

We are all like strangers in a strange country who seek understanding, and must look to Spirit for our guidance as our companions cannot teach us much. They are all working to set aside their own errors, that they may enter into their wonderful inheritance of understanding. We are all trying to become accustomed to the strange climate and temperatures, and the rules and law that we must obey.

The law is that every man speak only truth to his neighbor. Now the truth is always of the good and only the good; never a word of evil, for evil is not existent. But if we speak of what is called evil, the images we imprint upon the walls of the cave we form about us by so doing, come back upon us or reflect what seem hard and not good conditions.

To have understanding is to have knowledge of the Scripture writers and the meaning of their words. We find that they first told of the real and eternal and then of the unreal and temporal. In this way Moses first described the creation of the spiritual or real man and then the creation of the earth man or flesh. He says that the earth man was told that he could not know both good an evil. Spiritual understanding gives us knowledge of his meaning for it is true that while we know seeming evil we cannot know good, and on the other hand when we know good we have no knowledge evil.

In ancient symbology, good was wisdom, and evil was earthy or impure intelligence. Tree was but a symbol of knowledge. The tree of good and evil meant the union of wisdom and earthy intelligence of which man cannot partake and truly live. Serpent has always been a symbol of earthly wisdom, or the intelligence of sensuous thought. It was the sensuous (mortal) thought that tempted the earth man to believe that he could eat of both good and evil or wisdom and intelligence, which simply means that man cannot recognize or understand, cannot know or be, both Spirit and matter.

We are often told that we must not study shadows or talk about them, but we must know what causes a shadow in order to know the real from the unreal. A shadow is simply an obstruction of light. Substance cannot make a shadow, so it is something that has interposed between substance and light, and made his shadow called earth man – or flesh. It is the serpent of sensuous thought-or intellect-that obstructs the light of understanding; that thinks it is something of itself. We can remove this obstruction by denying the reality of intellect, for it is deceived into believing that all it sees is real, just as a room full of people were hypnotized by a fakir into seeing a tree grow up instantly from a seed. Even an artist drew a picture of the tree with his pencil. But a photograph of the room disclosed the fact that there was no tree there at all. We must train our intellect not to trust what its eye sees as none of it is true. We, as mind must be so sensitized (like the negative in the camera) by spiritual understanding that we report only real and true happenings. This can only be done by looking away from the obstacle that obstructs the light of understanding.

We have listened to intellect or mortal mind long enough and have had our reward in what we call evil. True mind understands the good only and knows that it has no shadow at all.

Carlyle said that the material world is a "shadow system gathered around our me," but he did not say that our "me" cast the shadow, for Reality cannot have a shadow at all.

It is sense thought that gathered the shadow system around itself thus keeping the light or wisdom from the me-the true creation. To be initiated into wisdom requires the struggle of casting out the dragon or serpent of earthly intelligence.

As shadows are nothing at all; only showing that the light is obstructed, so flesh is nothing but a showing forth of which tree we have eaten. If we have listened to intellect, the appearance-flesh-shows    restlessness,    wandering,    and homesickness, after the fashion of shadows; all is vanity, vexation, and ever changing conditions continually deteriorating until the shadow is gone. "All flesh is grass."

But when we understand the good, instead of the counterfeit flesh we have the real body-Spirit-sound and perfect in every part, indestructible and eternal. The true creation shines forth in all its glory, glorifying all about us.

Moses taught the sixth lesson in the words, "And God saw that it was good," meaning that immortal, eternal Mind understands only the good.

Jesus insisted that if we "seek first the kingdom of the good all things shall be added unto us." All who have sought and loved the good have proved this to be true, for they have had great power, to which all things and men were subservient.

Daniel and the three Israelites in the courts of the Chaldeans were proofs of this, for they loved God and the good in their companions and captors; they loved the lions, the fires, and all things till the fire of their loved melted all hatred, and all persecution, and took away from themselves all fear of anything whatever.

Those who thus love and understand the Good are at one with it by a state of the mind.

When we understand the Good and do not believe in any other power at all; do not shut ourselves up in a contracting room by speaking untrue words, we also will have great power; will have all power, for the I of us is like unto our Origin, Spirit-Substance-power, not only like unto this Omnipotence but one with it.

When we know that we are indeed one with God; of the same essence, substance; that there is no separation; that we show forth the works of God; prove that He does really work through us, then we have understanding. It is not the mortal that says, "I am one with God," but Spirit. Such understanding speaks forth words of power, and all shadows fall away revealing the new heaven and the new earth. The quickening irresistible Spirit is all, and its light breaks forth with love and healing. There is then no questioning of what is true. He who understands God knows all truth for the Christ has come to him, and Christ needed not that any man should teach him.

When we have understanding, or know that we are one with God and that God is everywhere and if that is true there is no disease anywhere in anybody. We know that we are health, and we need not even try to heal others, for as there are no opposites all who come near us are whole. Our realization of being one with all health is so strong that it heals, or our sense of the near presence of God who can be nothing but health, will heal all who come near or upon whom our thoughts rest.

John the revelator called the sixth foundation stone of the city of peace, "sardius"- "shining."

The sixth foundation stone in the study of Law is spiritual understanding. Did not the shining sardius point to this structure of peace now being erected for the sons and daughters of God?

The breastplate of judgment worn by Aaron, the first high priest of the Israelites, also contained the same stone- sardius. The sardius is one in the formation of rocks of all ages since the beginning of the visible world.

The word sardius has several meanings, one of which is above or beyond, and another, divine truth.

The breastplate also contained two stones or images (it is not certain which) called the urim and thummin. They signify light and truth or "the perfect light." The high priest believed that by gazing steadfastly upon these emblems, he received spiritual illumination; that the will of God thus became known to him. This was his way of consulting God.

When we have understanding we have entered into a new country, a city of peace. There are twelve gates to go through to obtain the knowledge necessary to claim our full inheritance. As we go through each gate we discover a different kind of fruit that we must show forth in ourselves, and to the world; for the perfect doctrine has twelve ways for us to practice and live.

Each fruit that we bring forth is controlled by a statement of this Divine Law, that we learn and practice, so that like the old astrologers we may call them the arbiters of our destiny-of twelve stars. As we go on studying and putting into practice these statements or rules we are building a perfect character, and each step that brings to fulfillment an undying virtue may be likened to a pillar. There are twelve pillars to uphold this perfect character, or the showing forth of eternal life.

Now when we have obtained the twelve baskets full of knowledge of Truth and Good they must overflow to all the world.

The miracle of abundant supply is ever being wrought, and we are ready and glad to assist in dispensing the bread of life to all who are ready to listen.

In this way we each become an high priest in the new city, with our feet set on the shining sardius red with living service for the world. It also shines from our breastplate of understanding, illumining our pathway with divine truth and pointing to the way above or beyond intellect. The "perfect light" of truth is our urim and thummim, upon which if we steadfastly fix our gaze, we shall surely have spiritual insight to guide us into the only knowledge that profiteth: The knowledge of the divine mind and of our oneness with it. In this way we have the only religion or the rebinding to God that the word religion signifies. It comes to us through the only wisdom or divine truth, and is the only atonement for sin, for it is the at-one-ment of God and man, making them of one mind. This is true understanding of Truth and God.

Let understanding speak forth the powerful words of truth. "Arise, shine for thy light is come." Nothing called evil can dwell where understanding of the presence of the good has flashed her glory over the face and spoken forth from the heart. All shadows must fall away, or all mortal conditions and ways. There is no night in truth understood. The eyes are opened to read wondrous things out of the law, for the book of life is an open book, and Spirit knows all things.

It is the "natural man" we read of in the book of life, or mortal man, the man of intellect, who knoweth not real things, "having the understanding darkened, being alienated from the life of God through the ignorance that is in them because of the blindness of their heart."

Those learned in occult lore, say that we are living in what they call a semispiritual cycle of time and are nearly at the close of it; that in six years a new cycle will begin which will be wholly spiritual; a reign of Spirit.

This seems quite reasonable for we all know that everything sweeps over the world in what we call waves. We are so enlightened that we know just what wave of weather or temperature to expect. Cyclones, tornadoes, disasters, crime, war, epidemics and financial troubles sweep the round earth. Shall we concede less to good than to what is called evil? Inventions, arts and sciences have their epidemics or crazes, and sweep the earth; literature becomes the rage and we call it a mental wave.

All things have come and gone in cycles and for quite a number of years there has been more attention given to the culture of the human mind than since the "golden age" of Athens. It is often spoken of as a mental wave. Is it not our golden age? And gold is but a symbol of good. What then more natural than to expect the next period to be one of good wholly and really; one in advance of all previous ones; a return to the paradise of Eden or garden of truth?

To be this it must be a spiritual reign, or wave, or cycle, whatever we choose to name it.

Occultists go on to say that materially minded people cannot breathe the coming atmosphere, as it will be too pure for them, just as the altitude of a very high mountain is dangerous for certain physical constitutions, and that all such will be annihilated by it. Possibly this fact is represented by the character and fate of, "She," for it was the immortal flame that consumed her.

If these prophesies are true to the world has but a short time in which to prepare for the new atmosphere-the new dispensation-and very few, comparatively, to show them the way into the new country and teach them how to become acclimated to the laws of the land.

Let us strive to hasten the day of our own understanding, and to help others all that lies in our power to reach the highest efficient shining forth of mind, or truth understood.

Let all go forth to rescue mankind from their delusions, panoplied with truth whose glad tidings of peace shall bear us up as on eagle's pinions. In one hand we shall have the sword of the word in the other the shield of faith. Covered with the robe of charity, girdled with the ephod of humility, adorned by the breastplate of love, and all surmounted by the helmet of trust in the Omnipresent Good.

By lowly listening we shall hear the promise repeated, "My presence shall go with thee and I will give thee rest." We have no need to seek this presence in a "pillar or cloud" or "bush of fire," for we *know* that God is everywhere and at all times as near to us as we are to ourselves.

This knowledge, or understanding, changes all of life to us. It wakes us from our dream of finding pleasure in material things. Fortunes may come and go without touching us for we know that God is our support and an unfailing supply and we shall never want for any good things.

Friends may stand or fail, we are undisturbed as they only prove themselves, and we love only the true, see only the true in all things and people. Storms of persecution may rage like electric storms, they cannot reach us, for a persecutor proves himself very mortal and we know only the immortal, we are free.

Heat and cold are alike to us, storm and sunshine, for we are in a country where the temperature is perfectly equable and the sun shines continually, as the presence of God is a brightness that the sun can never equal. Truly "One day in thy courts (spirit) is better than a thousand" in the world of matter (flesh). In thy presence "none of these things move me" for there is *only* God.

# NOTES

# NOTES

## The First Result of Knowledge.-The Origin of Man Explained.

We have had the six lessons concerning Principle; have explained Principle, or made the statement of Being; have given the rules by which to use Principle in directing our life, or solving its problem.

We have found that we must have faith in order to work well to reach the full understanding of Spirit. What is the first result of any knowledge that we acquire? Is it not to use it for the benefit of the world, thus fulfilling the law of love?

When we have knowledge of the Christ Science, the first thing to do is to follow His example and use it as He used His power, for this knowledge brings the same power to us that He had.

There are three ways of using this Science to bring health-which is but wholeness in every way, with happiness, which is eases, disease being only mind ill at ease showing out upon the body-"Who can minister to a mind diseased?" The understanding of Spiritual Law does minister to the human mind diseased, by teaching of the divine Mind which cannot be ill at ease poised, stayed forever upon its Author and Creator. Science teaches that the Real Mind-or Spirit-is perfectly wise, and free from any of those conditions we call mortal and hard; that all the thoughts of the True Mind are perfect, like unto the Creator in whose image and likeness true thought was made, and from whom it never departed for an instant. Thought has been hidden by the darkness of mortal ways and must now be brought forth-recreated by denying any other power except Spirit, or Divine Mind.

Our bodies show forth continually what our thoughts have been, just as the screen reflects the pictures that pass before it through the slide of a magic lantern, or as the retina of the eye takes the image of all the eye beholds. The mind is like an electric bell and each thought touches the button, which rings all through the body and life. A discordant thought will ring jarringly and harshly through the body, causing it to be out of order. If we gaze upon ugly objects they are impressed upon the retina of the eye and remain there for a long time to our discomfort. We say we are not able to get rid of the impression they felt. It is just so with thoughts. They are impressed upon the body and we cannot be rid of them except by replacing them by true good, ones. They show out as bodily pictures and we call them sickness.

The artist has the idea of his picture in his mind before he puts it upon the canvas, and if his ideas are ugly the pictures will be ugly also.

The body then is but a reflected picture. Thoughts are the things that are reflected and if they are true they reflect a true, whole and lasting body. To be true they must be spiritual like their Origin, Spirit.

If they are not true, not of Spirit, the body will be miserable, unenduring, and far from ease.

We can easily see then, why we have had sick and feeble bodies, for we know that mortal mind has told us falsely about our origin, and given us untrue beliefs regarding the real self of us.

We wish to work for others after we have trained our own mind according to the right rules. Then we must know the mistakes that all people hold in common, so that we can erase them from the mind of any who come to us for help, or that we have any desire to help whether they ask or not.

One who needs help has been trying to solve his problem with mortal mind rules, and as they are no rules at all of course they will not work correctly, so his calculations are wrong and he is paying the penalty by suffering and disease that will take his physical body out of sight.

When we know these universal false beliefs, we can use the rule of healing upon any conditions that they have brought to pass upon the body of any one who comes to us.

Whoever is bearing in his body the picture of false beliefs or thoughts; wants us to bring out his true self to the light of day; to open the windows of his soul by our true words, and let the light within spring forth to meet the light without: The spirit within through recognition will come forth to the Spirit that environs it gladly, and bring the holiness-wholeness-that was there from the foundation of all things.

This is no new doctrine, for Plato said, "Neither ought you to attempt to cure the body without the soul, for the reason why the cure of many diseases is unknown to the physicians of Hellas, is because they are ignorant of the whole, which ought to be studied also, for the part can never be well unless the whole is well."

All great students of mind or of human nature have said that mind is the cause of all material conditions.

Solomon said, "As a man thinketh so is he." Shakespeare

said, "There is nothing either good or bad but thinking makes it so." Mark Anthony said, "But, I unless I think what has happened is an evil, am not injured. And it is in my power not to think so." Ruskin said, "The men who look for the crooked will see the crooked, and the men who look for the straight will see the straight."

After students have listened to the first lessons of this Science (of Law), they generally feel disappointed and discouraged because they do not remember all that has been taught them, and they think they cannot work unless they can keep in mind all they have heard.

There is no need of being discouraged, though it is true that all the words are "drops of gold," for as we go on with the work we find that non one word is lost, and that we do recollect them as the opportunity presents itself for their use.

Have we not yet learned the law of eternal economy; that nothing is ever lost? Not only that, but truth multiplies seemingly, for there is always an infinite supply ready more than we need or can use. This the Science that Christ used, and with it we can always and at any moment feed multitudes.

The miracle of the loaves and fishes was but an illustration of the feeding of the mind with Truth, and an indication of Truth's inexhaustibility, for after we have received all we can use, have eaten enough, are filled, there are always twelve basketfulls left; always so much more than we can take.

Does it not seem a significant fact that fish and bread were used to typify spiritual food?

Spiritual food supplies the whole man-or mind-which makes its own body. In the language of mortal thought-the only language those fish-mongering people understood—fish supplies nutriment to the brain, which is supposed to be the seat of the mind; and bread to the body.

Was not Jesus proving that the food he gave- the spiritual sustenance-was to supply all needs, and did He not show that the supply was Infinite, far greater than any demand that could be made? Was He not proving what His Father was willing and ready to do and give?

We need feel no discouragement, for we have the same Father, whose supply is ever ready and always greater than any demand any number of His Children can make.

It seems strange, but not one word of Truth is ever lacking at our need if we trust. If we want a word for another, just wait a moment in the silence and it will come.

The twelve lessons are called twelve baskets full of eternal food-the bread and meat of Real Life.

They are also called the twelve foundation stones of the wall of the new heaven and the new earth, and the twelve gates of pearl through which we enter that are never shut to anyone. They are the twelve stars in the firmament of the law that when understood is sure to cast out the dragon of belief in evil-or mortal beliefs. When we truly know the law of Spirit we are sure to cry, "Now is come salvation, and strength, and the kingdom of our God, and the power of his Christ."

The Science of Spirit is the "pure river of the water of life with its trees bearing twelve manner of fruits," each leaf of which is for the healing of the nations, always yielding fruit.

Twelve must have been a very significant number to the Hebrews, for their history is full of the use of twelve.

The tribes of Israel were twelve. The sons of Jacob and the sons of Ishmael were twelve.

Moses built an altar with twelve pillars. The priest of the tabernacle wore a breast plate containing twelve precious stones. The children of Israel found at Elim twelve wells of water.

Twelve men bore the ark over the Jordan whose waters divided for them, and they took from the bed of the river twelve stones as a memorial of the event, and also set up twelve stones in the midst of the river.

Solomon's throne had twelve lions on each side of the steps, and the molten sea in his porch rested upon twelve oxen. The first appearance of Jesus in public was at the age of 12. Jesus had twelve disciples and there were twelve baskets full in the miracle of feeding. The visions of John are full of the number twelve. Twelve is the symbol of completion.

We find that mind is the cause of all material conditions, and that what we call mortal mind has created all the wrong or unpleasant conditions and environments.

Spiritual law will erase them because it erases the thoughts that created them, and this law is thoroughly scientific.

When the sun shines brightly overhead all the shadows are gone, so when the Spirit of us shines forth, the mortal creations which are but shadows that terrify our ignorance, depart.

In order to erase these beliefs that all have in common we must know what they are, as it seems a tendency natural to all to wish to help others.

Many people, perhaps the majority, are attracted to the study of Spiritual Law by the idea that there is healing for them. Everybody seems to need healing. But just as soon as they become thoroughly interested they forget all about self in their great desire to have others cured or benefited in some way. That is the time when their own real cure begins.

As we go on in the beautiful study we lose all thought of bodily conditions, caring only for spiritual advancement. This is the only real progress, and a truly spiritual state of mind will heal all who come in contact with us.

To attain to a spiritual life has been the aim of all the great of earth, always.

But the majority of mankind have been far from spiritual; so far, indeed, that they have always persecuted those who were so, and that is why we have such clouds of error to erase by denial.

The race has not even believed in their descent from God and that they were of the same substance with Him, Spirit, but have believed that they were created of and from and by flesh.

It is this very belief that made the race so material, so fleshly. And it is that we must deny till we are loosed from its bonds. We have believed that we can inherit sickness and weakness from parents and grandparents. It is a mistake and must be denied.

We make our own illness by the thoughts we think. If we have thought that we were wicked and sinful we have very likely been weak and languid.

If we have allowed temper to control our thoughts and

actions we have probably been dyspeptic or subject to violent colds.

If we have been deceitful, even in thought, it is not at all strange if rheumatism has seized us for its prey.

If we have been thoroughly selfish we need not be surprised if cancer makes its appearance.

Thus we find that thinking is serious business, and thoughts must not be allowed to run riot; must be harnessed and controlled as Plato's charioteer controlled his fiery steed while searching for wisdom and truth.

We must control thoughts by rejecting all that are untrue until it becomes easy to think only true ones.

This belief in flesh with all its attendant mistakes called lustful passions and sensual appetites, must be put out of mind as a first step in healing, or recreating the divine self of a patient.

There are six stages of this coming forth, and they may be slow in taking place or may demonstrate instantaneously. The slow changes are easily seen, and there is a rule to apply to each.

When we first hear of the necessity for denying sensual appetites and lustful passions in self or others, we think the words are out of place, are suggestive of degradation, and can have no place in the cause of our own troubles or of those we would help. This is from a misunderstanding of the words.

Sensual means "not spiritual or intellectual." Then has not the race need to deny sensual appetites, for do we not seem to live entirely in the senses, in gratification of fleshly or bodily desires?

It is this life, this mode of thought, that has brought all the trouble upon the race. Then if we strike the ax of denial at the root of the matter-the cause-the effect will be a change in conditions, proving our correctness of procedure. We shall thus erase the belief that satisfaction can be found in anything pertaining to flesh.

Lustful means "fleshly," so lustful passions are those pertaining to flesh. Have we not been expressly taught that we inherit avarice, greed, envy, hatred, malice, which are all but expressions of selfishness?

Has not our interpretation of "the sins of the fathers shall be visited upon the children," been that we inherit all fleshly appetites and misdemeanors?

As this is not true we deny it all, by the words rejecting sensual appetites and lustful passions, in order to erase the belief in all these particulars. There is no other way to be rid of them save by denial.

Does denial seem strange? Not when we stop to consider the important part it has had in the teachings of the church and of all great religionists. What is fasting but denial of self, or as it is called, "self-denial?" That this is considered a power by the church setting apart an appointed time for it and asking for "grace to use such abstinence, that, our flesh being subdued to the Spirit may obey the Godly motions."

Self-denial is simply renouncing fleshly gratification and all evil. "Renouncing the flesh and the devil," the church calls it.

To deny is only to forbid ourselves the indulgence of any appetite or desire; to give it up. And the more we deny the more we find we can do without.

In geometry, an occult line is a line that is necessary to the construction of a figure or problem, but is not intended to appear after the plan is finished.

In solving the life problem this occult line is denial, which is only obedience to an occult law. Occult is from a Latin word meaning 'to cultivate," and we can cultivate anything by reiteration.

We have seen persons who would tell an imaginary story until they really thought it was true. Repetition seems to be a force that changes our mind to agree with the words we repeat.

We can rid ourselves of any habit by constantly saying to ourselves, we will not do that. This is certainly denial, which is an occult law for cutting off-getting rid of-anything we desire.

The cultivation of this cutting off power which we call denial, has been carried to great heights, of which the history of the Church is filled with instances.

As we have said, there are three modes of healing according to Spiritual Law. The first and the one by which most healing is done is by adhering to given rules.

The second, is by the power which a trained mind has of detecting what error in thought is hidden cause of the sickness. This error, or belief, being wiped out by denial, truth give in its place, health shows out.

The third, and highest mode, is when we know truth so entirely, are so one with it, so permeated by it that our every thought is in accord with it, in fact we think nothing but truth, and our presence is sufficient to cure any malady. We do not need to be conscious of any attempt to help any one, but only love to all me that we wish all to be in truth. We are sure that God is ever near, and in His presence all are whole. This convictions carries great healing.

When we first set out to help our fellow men, not having this spiritual quality, nor intuition to perceive the special need of a patient, we must work according to a certain form that will cover all needs.

We must use rules before we can have realization of Spirit sufficient to cure. Rules train our own mind so that we can understand spiritually, or realize that health is indeed all there is. We must creep before we can walk. Paul said, "Hold fast the form of sound words." When we first try to cure according to Spiritual Law it is hard to understand the idea of addressing a person in the silence, if we know nothing of the law of the transference of thought. That we can really speak silently (mentally) to someone near or not near seems incredible to one who has not studied the law. If we do as we are told, however, no matter how blind we feel, we shall find that it will have an effect.

Do we ever stop to think how intimately connected all the people in the world are?

For instance, let one portion of the business world have a calamity, how quickly it is felt all over the world. How many are ruined by one failure in business circles. It is as if all were connected by an electric wire and all feel the shock of one touch up it.

Do we not always feel the force of a kind word, or of an unkind one? Cannot our whole be one of unhappiness caused by the remembrance of some  unpleasant remark early in the morning?

Will not a pleasant word and a warm smile make us happy all day? The wax in the audophone is not more impressible than the human mind. A glance, a tone, a smile, a word, even a movement, makes it lasting impression.

Cannot a glance be felt when we do not see the person who is looking at us? How often we have the same thought simultaneously with a friend and call it a coincidence. It is nothing of the kind, but it is the thought from one mind going to the other; being transferred. There is no limit to thought. It travels with the speed of the lightning. Can we not think of a friend in Europe as easily and quickly as of one close besides us?

Each receives our thought just as quickly as we can formulate it, and just as surely, and we may be very sure that each thought of ours reaches its destination.

Years ago, when inventions were not as plentiful as now, patterns of embroidery were obtained by means of impression paper (as it was then called), each lady tracing her own designs. Mortal mind is like the impression paper, and we are tracing our patterns upon each other continually; a thought is just as surely and easily impressed as a design upon paper may be.

Who can estimate the force of a kind word? It is said to heal a broken heart. Then what force a word of Infinite everlasting Truth must have. It is a great and important fact that not one word of Truth is ever lost, and when once placed in the mind of any one must work. We must be careful what words we speak; what thoughts we send forth.

The first time we tried this law of thought transference,

was to attempt to cure a headache. The girl was in an upper room, and in about fifteen minutes she came down free from her headache, saying, "Did you call me?" I think I fell asleep and dreamed that you called me."

We *had* spoken mentally and said, "You are well." This was proof to us that thoughts can go wherever we desire, so that we needed no argument upon the subject.

Whoever does not understand this law can prove the truth of it by trying in earnest and with faith. It is always doing that proves the doctrine, not hearing.

In order to show how healing is done we will take special notice of a person suffering as they suppose from asthma. We will say to her, mentally, but just as if we were speaking aloud, "You have no asthma and you could not inherit it as you have imagined, for you are not a child of flesh at all. You were born of Spirit-God.

"You are not subject to any law of heredity, for Spirit has no such law. The sensual appetites and lustful passions of mortality have not descended to you through parents and grandparents, to show forth as asthma. The whole race cannot cause you to have asthma, by its belief in fleshly conditions.

"Flesh is not the real of you and you cannot inherit what is not real. The asthma that you believe in is total unreality, for Spirit is never sick, therefore cannot give sickness or disease.

"Spirit-God-is Health itself, and you are one with this Spirit, therefore perfect health is yours. People near you cannot affect you by their beliefs in inheriting sensual appetites and lustful passions. You refuse to receive such ideas.

Your own passions and appetites cannot show forth as

asthma, for you are free from them because you are spiritually free from mortal conditions.

"I cannot affect you with any mortal thoughts or unconscious agreement with beliefs in lustful passions or sensual appetites. None of my errors can be pictured upon you as asthma. I withdraw all my false ideas of life, I do not believe in evil of any kind. You are Spirit, like God your Maker, and He made you whole and perfect, free from the flesh and all its ways. I believe you are wholly good.

"God is your life and it cannot be threatened with death nor fear death, nor yield to death, ever.

"God is your health and it cannot be threatened with sickness, nor fear sickness, nor yield to sickness at all.

"God is your strength and it cannot be threatened with weakness, nor fear weakness, nor yield to weakness.

God is your Peace and nothing can ever make you afraid. You cannot be disturbed by the fears of anyone living or whoever lived, no matter how much they believed in fear.

"God folds you round with peace and safety forever. You are sound and well in every part. You are perfectly well.

"You are alive with the Life of the Spirit; you are strong with the Strength of Spirit; you are bold with the Boldness of Spirit. You trust in God; you trust in God in every instant; you are perfectly well. You are ready to prove that you are perfectly well by acknowledging to all around you that you are perfectly well. You are willing to acknowledge to yourself that you are perfectly well. Your words shall establish this word of truth in a body free from false things. You are the perfect child of God who made you. You are a living witness of the power of Truth to set free into health and strength and living service for the world. Amen."

I am sure that being truth "my words shall not return unto me void, but shall accomplish whereunto I have sent them."

As has been said, one who is under the delusion of asthma, or any other malady, can be reached by such healing messages whether they are in Europe or right in the room with us.

Therefore we are taught to speak forth these ideas silently to all whom we wish to help, even while they are not present with us. Sometimes it has a wonderful effect upon a mind to repeat this beautiful treatment more than once. May be during the night while all is still and thoughts of God delight us most.

There used to be an old German practice of repeating silent messages three times at night, three times in the morning, and three times at night again. They performed wonders of healing.

Of course we understand why the repetitions were good. The mind actually gets to believing what it speaks often, and when it speaks truth till faith is aroused, that faith breaks down all barriers. By faith the very dead may be raised.

We have a right to have faith in the good for the good is true. There are thousands of people ready to testify to physical healing, heart comforting and mental quickening by the knowledge of Spiritual law.

# NOTES

# NOTES

# CHAPTER VIII

## Power of Law To Remove Deception.

The first result of knowledge of the Law of Spirit is to explain our origin, that we may understand that we are not under bondage to flesh in any way.

The second result, or second power of real law, is to remove from our mind the deception caused by a belief that we were born of flesh and can inherit fleshly conditions and appetites. We are commanded to "take heed to yourselves, that your heart be not deceived, and ye turn aside and serve other Gods, and worship them."

This command we have broken for we have turned aside from our God and believed in-worshiped- a God of evil. We have certainly bowed down to this God of evil and have been in bondage to it continually.

We have thus deceived ourselves, and our heart has been deceived by all our training, for evil is *not* true, of God is true, and is Omnipresence.

Two powers cannot inhabit the same space, so if God fills *all* space, evil is not anywhere.

As we said in the second lesson, we are all Mind like our Creator, but being inhabitants of earth we call our mind the earth mind.

This earth mind has been deceived by its earthly surroundings into believing that it is only earth-or flesh-and we must undeceive it by our only weapon-denial.

This earth mind says that the senses tell the truth when

when they form us that matter-flesh-is real and can feel.

But the senses deceive us when they tell any such thing, and if we agree with them we deceive other people. Jesus said, "Judge not according to appearances," and the senses are only appearances.

It is a sin to believe that evil is real, for it is having faith in another God beside the one true God. We must lay aside this sin and declare boldly that there is no reality in evil at all. Then the good will show forth. Good does not show out till we declare it, because we are deceived by the senses into believing that evil conditions are real.

It is not easy for us to leave off a long accustomed habit, but we know we can do it by persistent effort, even though the temptation to indulge the habit comes again and again.

Our false beliefs are like habits and must be denied any indulgence. We must say they are not true, and state what is true, that we may have something to lean upon after refusing the old props.

If we persist in saying there is no evil, we shall have our vision made clear to behold the good instead of what appeared to be evil-to see the silver lining to the cloud.

What we thought an evil circumstance will prove to brings us the greatest good. If what we call trouble brings us near to God- to a realization of the nearness of His presence-it is not trouble at all, but the greatest good that could come to us, for it is the path to God. It is the touch of the chord that vibrates from the finger of God.

He touches the keyboard and we respond. It is the silken cord that leads us out of the labyrinth of earthly woe.

If we were at a long distance from one we dearly loved would we think anything a trouble that we had to go through or overcome in order to reach the friend? Should we even notice our efforts? Our mind would be so riveted on the image of the dear one and the joy of the reunion, that we truly would not see or feel or know anything that transpired while we hastened toward his friend.

It is thus when we are with God, when we know God, feel His presence; we are only thankful for all that hurried or pushed us on to this moment, and can call it only good. We say truthfully, even in mortal language there is *no* trouble. It is the pathway to God, the silver line leading us out of the labyrinth of the mortal realm, out of earthly woe.

How often we have heard people say when things had not ended as they expected, "Well, it is best as it is after all."

Denial is a great power, for if we say there is no matter to a tumor, with persistence, it will disappear. We can say there is no matter until we do not see the people in a room, or a single object.

We can say there is no pain till all pain is gone, and other people's pain will go also, if we keep on saying this.

While we believe in evil we are keeping the good hidden from our experience, for we speak as we believe, and the law is that "by our words we are justified, and by our words we are condemned."

If God is Omnipresent and is Good itself and nothing else, then all the blessings we can desire must be in Him. We are told that "in Him we live, and move, and have our being," then are not the blessings very near us? Our eyes are holden by the beliefs in evil through which we have been deceived, and have deceived ourselves.

Students of to-day are not the first who have said that matter is unreal. All the wisest men of the earth have said the same, and it was the oldest teaching known. All the ancient philosophers taught it, and all modern ones, aside from materialists.

People report strange experiences from saying Spirit is all and matter is unreality, or from saying mind is all.

Some do not care to eat after making these statements; some do not sleep, and others wish to sleep all the time. Some have the old pains come back, and then are frightened. Many are afraid when they hear of these feelings, or are afraid when they have them. Others are afraid they may have something strange happen to them, so they dare not make the denials. mortal mind beliefs-especially the fears-are thus deceiving them into fear of truth itself, and keep them from seeing the good.

We can say from experience that there is nothing at all to fear.

Any strange experience or feeling is an indication that we have gone on from the old condition, into new powers, and are about to know greater truth. If we become afraid we keep ourselves from knowing this Truth that is ready for us, as there is nothing so clouding to the mind as fear.

We cannot be spiritual and mortal at the same time; either condition will prevent the other from showing forth.

While we are engrossed by mortal thoughts we know nothing of Spirit; it is a foreign clime to us; a rare atmosphere.

When people first go to Colorado they find the air so rare, so exhilarating, and withal so different from any they have been accustomed to, that they have great difficulty in breathing, and often feel smothered. After they have stayed there for a time all unpleasant feelings pass away, and they are stronger, better than ever before in their lives, because they are breathing purer air than ever before.

When people go to the top of Pike's Peak they suffer greatly from the same cause. The pure air suffocates, stifles, even stops the beating of the heart, makes the nose bleed, causes deafness and blindness, and some are temporarily insane.

Does all this general experience deter visitors from going to the top? Not often, though there may be some who would not risk such experiences for a sight of all the grandeurs and sublimity of scenery in the world. There are always some who are afraid of their own shadows.

Entering upon a spiritual life is just like climbing this mountain, or like inhabiting a new, pure climate. The rare, pure atmosphere created in and around us by a coming forth, a regeneration of the spirit we are beginning to recognize, causes just such a stirring up of mortal tendencies, just such a disturbance.

As soon as we declare that we are Spirit instead of matter, that declaration purifies our inward atmosphere to a certain extent, and pure air and impure air can never occupy the same space; one must retreat, being overpowered by the other.

If the unreal, untrue, impure, or matter, makes a

disturbance as the physical body does in going up the mountain, shall we go down to the level plain again, and give up our hope of seeing the promised grandeur, our hope of satisfaction, of harmony, or heaven?

All these feelings are but signs that we are ascending into an atmosphere that will be permanently beneficial, of everlasting purity and strength. They prove that we are approaching unknown heights, where none of these things can affect us when we have become acclimated.

Is it not considered a law of physical life that if we go to a strange country we must become climated? And what does that mean?

Why, to go through some new experience, some change is bodily conditions that are from pleasant, are often distressing.

If the country is one that we very much desire to live in, do these experiences drive us away, or keep us from going there? No, indeed.

Does a real artist ever stay away from Rome for fear of the Roman fever he is quite sure to have? Is a missionary ever deterred from going to Africa on account of the effect the climate is almost sure to have upon him, sooner or later? Did fear of pain or danger ever keep a gold seeker from California, or a diamond seeker from the mines of Australia?

Nothing of value was ever attained without effort and struggle, and some things that are unpleasant to mortality.

It is a new country we enter when we learn that we are Spirit, and as we obey the laws of that country they are so foreign to mortal ways that we feel the effects, the stir, made by the mortal in becoming accustomed to new ways of thinking.

For instance, we learn that as Spirit, we can never be impatient or uncharitable, and this may cause a great change in our habits.

Perhaps we have been very critical of people and their ways when they differed from ours, and thought we could not help being provoked when there was just provocation. Now we must suppress not only the outward semblance of anger or impatience, but actually stifle the feeling; not allow it.

It is held by those versed in physical laws that suppressed anger is very injurious to the system, so will it be any wonder if we are made ill when we first try to drive out all such feelings?

According to science, thoughts of anger indulged are pictured out upon the body as rheumatism or dysperia. So even after we set out for the new country our past thoughts may show forth upon the body, until we have well denied the power of mortality and declared the truth that makes free.

Now if we willingly undertake and risk the suffering from a change in mortal life simply for the gratification of the senses are we unwilling to become acclimated in the new country that is an heavenly one?

Can we not see all pains and so-called hindrances as but steps on our road, rounds of the ladder, each one bringing us nearer the promised land of beauty unsurpassed, happiness undreamed of? *Can* we call these steps evil? Can we help crying aloud for joy at each, because we are one step higher? Are they not signs of good to us?

Should we not be glad to be so sure that we are in the new country, knowing by the signs that we are sure to be rewarded a thousand fold for any experience we may be tempted to call disagreeable?

A change to mortal ways is always a shock, but it is for our highest good; then is not good? We must not be deceived into calling the evil real. No, it is the real that is coming to us by means of the change that causes the showing forth temporarily of these seeming unpleasantness.

The truth will set us free from these very conditions we call evil, if we cling to it. The truth is that we are Spirit and not mortal. Can Spirit feel pain, or heat or cold? No. Then if we are sure that we are Spirit, we know that none of these things can affect us. What we declare shows forth.

We must not listen to the intellect, for it does not tell truth. It agrees with the senses, and they are not true, as we know. All that we see with the physical eye must be denied if it interferes with us or seems to do so. We must declare it unreal whether it interferes with us or not, that we be not deceived.

Nothing that we see is real, it is only the semblance of reality. The idea expressed by it is the reality.

Paul said to the Galatians, "Be not deceived; God is not mocked: for whatsoever a man soweth, that shall he also reap."

He tells them that they who sow the flesh shall reap of the flesh, and they who sow to the Spirit shall of the Spirit reap everlasting life. And he told them that if they would 'walk in the spirit" they should "not fulfill the lusts of the flesh."

Then if we think that any good thing can come of flesh we are deceived.

John tells us that "many deceivers are entered into the world who confess not Jesus Christ," and that "he that abideth in the doctrine of Christ, he hath both the Father and the Son."

Then we must infer that whoever has the perfect doctrine of Christ is not deceived, and that all others are deceived.

Jesus said, "Flesh profiteth nothing," so if we believe in flesh or mortal ways as real, we are deceived.

John saw in his vision the destruction of the city of evil, and said, "By the sorceries were all nations deceived."

He shows the utter futility of all things mortal and fleshly; all that mortal man calls good.

Then if we believe in these we are deceived, and if we allow any one who so believes to influence us in any way we allow them to deceive us.

If we are deceived we must be in bondage. All mortality is bondage, and its varieties are many and subtle. One of the most subtle is fear.

Mortal mind is in bondage to a multitude of fears, and one that is a source of great trouble to many is called by several names: Mesmerism, psychology, animal magnetism, or its most fashionable appellation, hypnotism.

It is the influence- as they believe of one mortal mind over another, and their want of faith in the Christ doctrine, they fear this. Perfect faith casts out doubt, and fear is but doubt of the one true power. It is really their ignorance of the subject that makes them fear its influence; they are deceived through their own ignorance into fear.

When people fear anything at all why do they not seek for information upon the subject and see if there is really any cause for their fear, or if they have conjured up a bugbear through want of accurate knowledge? Instead of this they take the word of some one equally as ignorant as themselves, who tells them that such a person has a malicious influence over people by thinking thoughts of error toward them, or that people are so infatuated by such and such a person that he must use undue influence."

'Who is this that darkeneth counsel by words without knowledge?"

Is not this exactly the same kind of a scare that caused the unjust executions of people called witches on Boston Common? Are we willing to return to such barbarity, even in thought?

Is it not the same that the ignorance of the colored race calls "hoodooing? Are we willing to be classed with such ignorant people?

To begin with, all who fear these things are utterly wrong, even from a material standpoint. If they will carefully peruse the scientific investigations that have been made into these things by competent judges they will find that all the 'semblance of power exerted by one individual over another has been traced to the brain of the subject, acted upon from without, by suggestion through impressions previously made."

Braid's method of hypnotizing was "by giving a particular direction to the subject's imagination; by concentrating the attention upon an arbitrary point or raising an image of the sleep in the subject's mind, which is most easily done by speech. He considered the steady attention and steady gaze of the subject indispensable."

"The Abbe Faria, from India, showed by experiments that no unknown force was necessary for the production of phenomena in mesmerism. The cause of the sleep, said he, was in the person who was to be sent to sleep. All was subjective. This is the main principle of hypnotism.

All these are noted authorities upon the subject of mesmerism or hypnotism.

Did we never cause a lady to blush by simply suggesting to her that she was blushing? That shows the force of an idea suggested to the mind. The idea that is to mesmerize one must be deceived into the mind of that one, or it cannot be done.

We must be receptive of the ideas or they will not affect us.

All of Mesmer's pretensions when scientifically examined into were found to be of no avail unless the patient expected to be magnetized. The decision was that "the effects actually produced were produced purely by the imagination of the patient."

An eminent authority says, "The phenomena of hypnotism clearly arise from the physical and psychical condition of the patient and not from any emanation proceeding from others."

This all applies to the new scare about the thoughts of affecting us, and we commend the wisdom of Pope to all who have this fear. 'A little learning is a dangerous thing."

If we expect the thoughts of others to hurt us and are always fearing them our expectant attention will have its reward, but it will be our own fears that hurt us. We mesmerize ourselves by fixing our mind upon the supposed harm. Job said, "The thing I feared is come upon me."

Others do not think about us as much as we imagine. We are not so important in their estimation as in our own; leaving material science for the science of the Spirit, the true explanation of this great fear, we find it more unfounded still, for if we are established in truth not all the powers of mortal mind in the body or out can influence or affect us. If mortal thoughts affect us it proves that the people who send them are stronger in their beliefs than we are in the truth.

Nothing can prevail against one panoplied in truth. "If God be for us who can be against us?"

One who believes he is influenced by others forgets his birthright; forgets that he is the child of God and free from all evil.

We have a key that will open our mansion in our Father's house. It is this word, *I am free because God made me in His own image: I am wise in truth, and I am immortal.*

Mansions are states of mind, this key is the open sesame to each state of mind wherein is safety. Is not a man foolish to throw away such a key, or forget it? We also have a weapon of defense against all influences that are not true. It is, "one of these things move me" because I am hid with Christ in good.

If we say, I am mesmerized or magnetized by someone's thoughts, we are throwing away both key and weapon, and not only that, but it shows a lack of faith in the power of God. If He is the only power all these things are nothing and it is impossible for them to affect us.

How can we fear if we believe that God is near, and believe in His omnipotence? Fear is doubt of God's power.

No one can use our key for us. We are told that "every man shall bear his own burden;" and that "a man's word in his only burden." Then all rests with the word we use, and when we know the true words, if we allow ourselves to be deceived is it not our own fault?

If, instead of trying to think who has sent us thoughts that bring pain and trouble-or what has been called "malicious animal magnetism"- we would search our own thoughts for some uncharitable one that has gone out, it would be more to the purpose, for every one we send forth comes back upon our own head with unerring certainty.

Holding such thoughts for even a moment changes the condition of the blood. Jesus said, "First cast out the beam from the thine own eye." If we follow this advice we shall be very busy and have no time to see or think of our neighbor's motes.

Spiritual law teaches ' the charity that *thinketh* no evil," and if we would only live according to its precepts and rules we should never be deceived into fear of sickness or any belief of evil.

In healing anyone we must reject all deception, whether their own or that handed down from parents and grandparents, or by reason of the whole race, or the deceptive notions of friends and neighbors. As they do not understand how to do this for themselves, we do it for them when they appeal to us for help.

In the last chapter we gave helpful thoughts to one who

believed in asthma. That one could not help feeling freer and more hopeful. Often such a thought makes them quite well. We must now remove deception from their mind, if we see them not entirely relieved, by saying, "You have not been deceived into thinking that you have asthma. I do not believe in deception. You have not inherited the consequences of deception, because you came forth from Spirit and not from matter. The whole race mind cannot deceive you and it has not deceived you into such an error as thinking you have asthma. You know that you live and move have being in God. You are surrounded by Spirit and love, not by mortality and hate, so truth shines over you, and not error. Therefore you are well. Listen to me; I tell you the truth; you are not deceived or mesmerized. You cannot be deceived. Rise and assert your own independence of mortal mind. Stand out free in Spirit. Your friends and neighbors cannot influence you into believing what is not true. What do you care for the opinions and thoughts of people, when you are wise with spiritual judgment? You cannot be self-deceived, no self-deception or self psychologizing ever affects Spirit. Spirit is free, wise and immortal. I have no mental quality which deceives you, or mesmerizes you into having asthma seem a reality. I do not, and I will not, let any child of God suppose false things by my own false sights and fears. I leave you free to know that because God is your life it cannot be threatened with death, nor fear death, nor yield to death, ever.

"God is your health; it cannot be threatened with disease or sickness, nor fear disease or sickness, nor yield to disease or sickness, ever

"God is your strength; it cannot be threatened with weakness, nor fear weakness, nor yield to weakness, ever.

"God is your peace; it cannot be threatened with discord or inharmony, nor yield to discord or inharmony ever. You have perfect peace in the security of God's watchful care over you, and around you forever.

"You are sound well in every part. You are perfectly well.

"You are alive with the life of the Spirit; you are strong with the strength of the Spirit; you are bold with the boldness of the Spirit.

"You trust in God, and trusting in God you are perfectly well.

"You are ready to prove that you are perfectly well by acknowledging to all around that you are perfectly well.

"You are willing to acknowledge to yourself that you are perfectly well. You are ready now to acknowledge to me that you are perfectly well.

"Your own words shall establish this word of truth, in a body free from false things.

"You are the perfect child of God who made you. You are a living witness of the power of truth set free into health and strength and living service for the world. "Amen."

When she is gone, I decree that my words shall not return unto me void, but shall accomplish whereunto I have sent them.

Many people have seen all the perfection of their sick neighbor at once, and so that perfection has shown forth at once. In speaking the wonderful truth of the Spirit to the "natural world" or deceived mind, this truth takes away troubles as the daylight chases away phantoms.

Some reasoners think along the steadfast lines of spiritual law to the disorderly mentality around them. In refusing to believe in our neighbors' being under the bondage of lustful passions, sensual appetites, deceptions, Mosaic science has given us a key to correct order.

Whichever way we think we are sure to see pictured around us. Therefore we think truly and are wise in words.

# NOTES

# NOTES

# CHAPTER IX.

### Power of Law To Annul Sin.

When we understand a law, that law gives us knowledge of certain things, which if we act in accordance with will bring certain results.

Now the law of the Christ will bring perfect health and happiness-or satisfaction-if we use the knowledge it conveys in an orderly way.

The first step in understanding this law explains the origin of the race and its mistake concerning birth.

The second power of understanding this law removes from the mind the deception resting upon the race concerning the heredity of sickness and trouble.

The third power in the law is to destroy the false idea concerning sin and its effects upon the race. The race has been taught to believe that it suffers for the sins of the first inhabitants of the earth-according to most ancient tradition-and also, for the sins of immediate ancestors, as well as for each one's own.

This has made a heavy burden to bear, and it is no wonder that the result has been sickness, discouragement and despair.

If a man were condemned to carry upon the top of his head a heavy iron weight all his days would he be apt to desire the days to be long or many? Would he be cheerful and happy ever? Would he not rather long for death to end physical suffering?

The race has borne, is bearing, this burden of iron upon

head and shoulders, and the true science comes to lift it off and give freedom, that people may stand erect as becoming men and children of God.

This belief in sin and the necessity through heredity, of sinning, has been received because man has not known his true origin as Spirit and sinless, but believed he was flesh and "prone to err as the sparks to fly upward."

The universal desire to get rid of this conviction of sin has filled the world with religions of all kinds. Men have sought for some means to be rid of sin by penance, or sacrifice, or work, or faith, or some invention by which they might atone, and yet there is one noticeable fact, they have still clung to their wrong doing. They would do anything except actually give up sinning.

The truth is, that man is one with is Creator. Can that Creator sin or know sin? Any one will answer no. Then the true man cannot know sin and is not flesh. He has made unto himself a body of flesh, by having fleshly thoughts and beliefs, which flesh is only an intimation of the real body. If he will have only spiritual thoughts his body will show forth what it really is, spiritual and perfect. The one perfect man-and our example-had only a spiritual body, for did it not enter a room with windows and doors closed? To know who we are is to begin to bring forth this spiritual body, and as it comes forth it drives away the body of flesh, which is the shadow of mortal thoughts, because Spirit takes the place of that intellect which obstructed the light of Spirit by showing what we called a shadow-or flesh. Intellect is not a power, is not reality; it is only an intimation, a counterfeit of spiritual intelligence. Does not counterfeit money always produce a disturbance when found out to be such, and is it anymore a reality for that fact? No. It is nothing at all, and never can be anything but an intimation. And so is intellect, with its shadowy body, nothing at all.

Spirit is all there is, in reality. But the unreal intellect has made such a miserable body that everybody is interested in wanting to change its conditions, and this interest is paramount to every other. Health is the cry, the great desideratum of all mankind. It is the elixir of bodily life they have ever sought.

A whole body is inseparable from Spirit, Soul, Mind, and how strange it is that people have been so deaf to this fact when it has been taught and told over and over again.

But mankind has been so fleshly and so proud and vain of his intellect, that these ideas have been scoffed at as transcendental; they are beyond the scope of intellect, beyond its power of comprehension, hence it rejects them as absurd.

These truths have been advocated repeatedly, but their advocates have been crushed, or persecuted and mocked, and their ideas sneered at by the "foremost intellect of the age" in which appeared.

But now they are gaining a widespread credence, because people are tired, weary, of all the old ways of getting a health which does not last. In the majority of cases where people first study this law, it is for its power of bodily healing, so much we do as a race care for bodily comfort; even more than for mental endowments, and far more than for spiritual development.

We seem to think that Spirit will develop when we have cast off the body; that this body trammels Spirit in its development.

All this comes from the belief in sin, or that we are sinful and miserable creatures. While we believe this we think and speak slightingly of God our Creator, because all that He created He "saw that it was good," and He "made man in His image," therefore perfect like himself.

Suppose an extremely beautiful person were to go about deeply and heavily veiled always, could we know anything of the hidden beauty?

We hide our perfection under a heavy veil of mortal belief in sin. We must tear off this veil by denial and disclose to our own selves our true character, our perfection, our real being-Spirit.

Let the senses report what they will, we must not heed the, for they are not true reporters. We must stifle all that tells us that what we see, or hear, or feel physically, is true, and then we shall leave the real seeing, hearing, and feeling free to tell us the truth.

What Spirit tells us is true, and we must believe it all the time, not at one time and then at another return to our beliefs in evil.

Truth will not have a divided service and give us the beast and highest demonstrations.

If people talk of sin, sickness, and trouble, we must deny (mentally) the truth of their words, keeping our mind's eye on the real, which is Spirit-sinless and well. Spirit cannot see imperfections. It is the mortal mind, which in reality is no mind at all, only a claim to be something, that sees evil things, The real mind is never separated from its Creator and it thinks

God's thoughts.

We must hold to this truth for each thought that arises from this is full of power because it is a right thought, and right thought is righteousness.

Solomon said, "The mouth of a righteous man is a well of life,"

David said, "God will never suffer the righteous to be moved." Then righteousness, or right thought is power and safety.

What we call sins are but mistakes we make in our seeking the good. We are all seeking satisfaction and it only rests in the good, but not knowing this we seek in various ways for it, and these are our mistakes. These mistakes are the stumbling block of iniquity spoken of by Ezekiel. 'These men have set up their idols in their heart, and put the stumbling block of their iniquity before their face; should I be inquired of at all by them?"

The idols set up, are beliefs in an evil power; for that is idolatry as God is the only power. The stumbling block of iniquity is belief in sin, for while we believe we must sin, how can we inquire of God's ways?

Before we can understand the good we must wash out our mistakes and beliefs by denial, and forsake them by clinging to true thoughts. What we call evil things are but signs that the Spirit is breaking forth, and is pushing out the mistaken thoughts and their fruits upon the body. They are in reality signs of good.

It seems hard to believe that all we do not like, all that seems unendurable, is good, but if we cling to true words we shall see it so at last. For the undendurable is not there at all in reality. The Substance working with us is the good only. Sometimes it seems to people as if there is so much to learn concerning spiritual law that they never can know all they ought to know about it. "Patience and perseverance accomplish all things." When we understand the principle, the rules and laws are easy of application, if we persevere. We need only to understand what we are doing and keep steadily and firmly to our work, to win.

If we tell someone (mentally) that they are not in pain, the whole attitude of their mind disputes it, but we must keep on, till unconsciously they accept our statement in mind, and all pain is then gone.

If we have the pain when it leaves that one, it shows that we are not strong in truth and we must deny that we can take the thought that caused the pain. We simply exchanged ideas, sending them one of health and they sent us their pain producing one. We must be stronger than that by saying before we think of anyone, that as Spirit we cannot be affected by any mortal mind at all. Then keep to our declaration that there is no pain at all, anywhere.

When we speak mentally to a person according to the law of Spirit we do not try merely to remove the physical pain, for that is but the sign of what is going on in the mortal or natural mind. We attend to thoughts only and if we know him well enough to know the prevailing thought that is being pictured upon his body, we erase that thought and implant a true one instead.

If we do not know him well enough for this, and

if we have not spiritual intuition to perceive what it is, then we must go according to the rule and speak to the thoughts and beliefs common to the whole race. This drives out *all* thoughts of error.

If we are faithful he will get rid of his diseases as people say. But it is just being rid of those false thoughts that were the sole cause of disease. The disease is only the representation of the thought held in mind, just as the picture is the representation upon canvas of the artist's idea or thought. When artists used to allow their thoughts to dwell upon hell and demons they produced some horrible pictures. We do the same when we think upon sins in ourselves or others, and our bodies are the canvas upon which we paint our pictures.

For instance, suppose we have been trained from infancy to fear cold and heat, and to be careful of our diet for fear certain kinds of food would make us sick, or to fear epidemic and disaster, by the time we arrive at an age of responsibility, we fear for self and others till fear is our prevailing state of mind.

After we learn the law of science we know that the only cause of any pain we may have is fear, not cold or heat or food, so we deny that a child of God can know fear at all, for as we live and move and have our being in God, we breathe from Him nothing but courage, and are filled full of courage.

After this declaration, any pain we have we must assert is the fear being driven out by the courage we constantly breathe, and thus is not an evil but a sign of good; is not pain but a sign of health; is not weakness but a sign of strength; or we may say, it is strength pushing out fear.

These mortal states are but sign-posts on the road to rest and health, showing us which way to go and how far we are on our way.

All the old ways of trying to find health have failed, because there is but one health and that is God-Spirit.

God is not in material things, therefore while we sought in them for health we did not find it. They are but temporary reliefs. Simply patching an old garment, and we know that if we attempt that, just as fast as we put a patch on one worn spot another place gives away, till if we go on there will be nothing but patches. Is it not exactly so with the body all through mortal life, as fast as we get one thing healed by material methods do we not find another pain to work upon and fret over?

We must exchange the old garment for a new one, instead of making it all patchwork, and so we must exchange our old mortal body for a new one, a recreated one-in God.

Recreated by our right thoughts, for *we* make our bodies, God did not. He can only make Spirit, and we as Spirit have our own work to do; our own creating, or manifesting of the perfect creation, which is of one substance with the Father.

Now, as we do not know to what special belief a strange person has been trained, and we do know that the whole race has been taught to believe that sin holds them in its chains, and they must suffer for it, we can name over the different sins believed in by all, and when we have it upon the one that the patient believes he is guilty of, his disease will loose its hold, if we deny the sin.

We must first name and deny each one, for not one

has any influence over the child of God-who is Spirit only.

We will take that one who has asthma and apply this rule if she or he has the idea in mind that sin caused the asthma, saying decidedly:"If all mortal mind claims that you have asthma, as mortal mind itself is only terror, so all its beliefs are error, and you cannot reflect any idea that is not true.

"Even parents in flesh, believing themselves selfish, envious, jealous, malicious, revengeful and cruel, cannot bring asthma to you, and you had no parents in the flesh, for you-the real you-are spiritual, not material.

'Selfishness-envy-jealousy-malice-revenge-cruelty-are the sins the race believe in, but such beliefs from the whole race cannot bring upon you asthma, or influence you at all. The race law is annulled. You are free from mortal mind influences for you are not material, but spiritual.

"All your friends and neighbors cannot influence you to believe in mortal influences, thus bringing upon you asthma. All their beliefs in the power of sinfulness cannot affect you, for you are free with the freedom of the Spirit.

'The belief in your own sins has no power over you. Listen to my words: You are not selfish-you are not envious-you are not jealous-you are not malicious, revengeful or cruel, therefore you cannot have asthma. You are not mortal, and therefore not sinful at all. You are the perfect child of God, sinless and free.

'My mortal belief in sin of any kind cannot stand between you and the true words I speak to you, for these sins do not belong to me. I deny them and deny any belief in them at all, so they cannot reflect upon you to harm you.

"You are free from all belief in sin, and are whole and at peace.

"God is your life and it cannot be threatened with death, nor fear death, nor yield to death ever.

"God is your health. It cannot be threatened with disease or sickness, nor fear disease or sickness, nor yield to disease or sickness at all.

"God is your strength. It cannot be threatened with weakness, nor fear weakness, nor yield to weakness.

"God is your peace. It cannot be threatened with discord or inharmony of mind or body, nor fear discord or inharmony of mind or body, nor yield to discord or inharmony of mind or body ever.

"You are perfectly sound and well. You are alive with the life of Spirit; you are strong with the Strength of the Spirit; your trust is in God.

"You are safe and free. You are perfectly well, because God made you.

'Acknowledge to all around you that you are perfectly well. Acknowledge to yourself that you are perfectly well. Acknowledge to me that you are perfectly well.

'Speak the truth from this time forth- that you are Spirit, whole and sound and perfect."

This cleansing from the belief in sinfulness sometimes makes the cure seem to take longer, but it is the perfect healing when it is accomplished.

The denial of disease has temporarily cured many. The denial of sin is the permanent cure of all.

"Cleanse thou me from secret faults."

If "envy is the rottenness of the bones," as Solomon discovered, you can plainly see that the bones cannot be well till there is no envy anymore forever.

The denial of the reality of envy is like a moral bath. Ezekiel tells of the cleansing waters which God washed the Israelites within olden days, it is prophesied that He would in the last days cleanse the world so that the inhabitants should "not say I am sick anymore."

# NOTES

NOTES

## Fourth Power of Law.

In studying the law of Spirit and the efficacy of its spoke word, we learn of its wonderful power to remove from what we call mortal mind its erroneous ways of thinking, giving in place of mistakes, truth.

Truth is powerful; truth is powerful itself. It is the Spirit of God, "moving upon the face of the waters" of the changeable human thoughts, and as Paul expressed it, is the 'Spirit bearing witness with our spirit that we are the children of God."

Now if we are ready and willing-or glad to receive words of truth like little obedient children, we shall drink them as the buds raise their heads for the downfalling of the dew, each petal receiving according to its need, till it blossoms into full glory and fragrance.

The Spirit falls over us as gently as the dew, and if we receive it graciously and gratefully, opening the petals of our mind, we shall blossom as quietly as the rose and shed abroad the unmistakable influence of the Spirit, till all will know that we have walked with God.

But if we are like a refractory child who will not listen to its mother's kind, wise counsels, but opposes everything she says, thinking itself far wiser than mother, we shall, like the child, go on in our mistakes more blind than ever, until we are so torn in the conflict that we come back to the ever patient Mother-Spirit and meekly listen to its words for our guidance.

The word of truth is like a sword. A sword is a valuable weapon in skilled hands but a dangerous plaything. If we quietly let the sword of the word do its work with ourselves it will cut its way straight through mortal ways if thought sending errors to right and left without disturbance; but if we oppose it at every step it will cut and wound us for our stubbornness.

A sword that cannot go straight must glance off in some direction and its work is thus impeded or obstructed.

What is the state of the rebellious child? Is it not restlessness, excitement, irritableness and anger against all the kind words of its mother?

Well, this is just the state of our mind if we oppose true words, or will not listen to them. The tumult in mortal mind caused by opposing truth has given rise to the comparison of truth to a chemical process.

Error is like a powerful acid. Now we all know the effect of acids. Anyone who has tried to remove iron rust from table linen with salts of lemon (oxalic acid) knows that if the crystals are left too long in one spot a hole is the result. The acid burns the linen away, or in common parlance, "eats it up."

Now oxalic acid-a-deadly-poison-is made from something that seems very harmless; something that every country child knows and eats, viz., the plant oxalis, or sorrel with its pleasantly acid leaves.

Probably, if a child should eat nothing but sorrel leaves the acid would become concentrated enough to destroy the body. Exactly so a little error seems very harmless but it concentrates into an acid that destroys.

This is the state the race has been in since its beginning in error, and the acid of its errors has been the destroying agent that has filled what we call "the cities of the dead."

But we have a remedy for all this, just as chemistry has an antidote for the acid. An alkali neutralizes or destroys the effect of acid by causing it to change its base entirely. The alkali is caustic, burning, cutting, pungent-and converts the acid into an entirely new compound, which is harmless.

The true word has been compared to an alkali, because it does the same work upon mortal mind, or error, that the alkali does with the acid. Truth is caustic, sharper than a sword, pungent or searching, and does its work as relentlessly as the alkali, converting the error into a new compound, or changing its base.

If we receive the truth as gladly as we would take the antidote for chemical poison, the change will be painless, but if we try to refute or contradict each word of truth we hear, we shall be in the condition a man would be in who should fight against talking the antidote to the poison acid. His pains would increase.

Does it seem reasonable that hearing about God who made us and loves us and who could create only good, should cause a fermented state of mind or thought?

It certainly should not, and never would if mortal mind was perfectly poised; if it did not cling to its errors, resisting the truth that will set it free. If we would be quiet and say to the Spirit, "Search me and try my thoughts," and then gladly deny every error as it presents itself in thought, we should feel no disturbance; each error would quietly, noiselessly, harmlessly, be thrust out.

The truth does search ever corner of the mind and reveal everything that is hid or covered, and as we gladly let go of each error we take a step up and on. It is truly "stepping heavenward"-into harmony.

We are indeed going home to our father's house and each day can say, "Nearer my home to-day than ever I've been before."

The change was made in us and made effectually but also imperceptibly, because we resisted not. Is it not a wonder that the change should ever cause any disturbance of mortal mind?

But it certainly does, and as truth has been compared to one chemical (alkali), and error to another (acid), the change which the attempt to mix them causes, is called "chemicalization."

Neither Webster nor chemistry, has such a word, but it is very expressive of the state, and was probably coined from the word chemistry, meaning, "the laws of combination and charge of substances, or chemical change."

When we wonder that anyone can be disturbed by the change caused by truth, it is because the scope of our observation of human nature has been small and our own experience has been such as to make us ready to receive the words, as the parched traveler drinks, unquestioningly, only caring that the thirst is quenched.

Mortal mind is so accustomed to routine of thought that if a sudden change therein is presented, a shock is often the result; for instance, we may be in a very placid frame of mind and let someone tell us what we call bad news, what a chaotic condition we are at once plunged into; or let one tell usunexpected good news and how excited or stirred up we feel.

What power there is in words. How often a striking discourse, or one setting forth an unwonted train of ideas, will give us a sleepless night. We turn over and over the thoughts that rush through the mind till our heads feel in a whirl; or some spoken words touch a chord that vibrates, disturbing the harmony of the whole mind. Even an insinuating tone of voice will do this, or something implied though not said. Suppose we find out that one we deemed true is treacherous? Does it not cause a disturbance in our thoughts that it takes some time to quell? Is not all this like fermentation which must subside we are again calm and steady?

The mind is like a delicate instrument which a breath of air will affect, unless we know how to use and control it. A physician said that "the brain of man is so nicely and delicately balanced that the least shock disturbs its balance, and, consequently, not one in a thousand is perfectly poised or balanced."

This is the condition of mortal mind, for it is so wedded to its old ways of thought that the truth shocks, unbalances it, causing a commotion or fermentation and a persistent attempt to return to or cling to error. It is like a liberated prisoner who cares nothing for pure air and freedom; indeed, does not understand them, and prefers his cell to them.

Habit is so strong in mortal mind. Dickens illustrated this aptly in the story of the man incarcerated in the Bastile, who had spent twenty years making shoes. At the time of his imprisonment the chord of love for his wife and child received a violent shock and after his liberation, whenever that portion of his life previous to the incarceration was spoken of, the same chord was jarred and he returned to his shoemaking supposing that he was again a prisoner.

Thus do we cling to old habits of thinking, to errors, and we find it is not quite so easy to control our thoughts as we imagined when first told how potent every thought is for good or for seeming evil.

A true word is like a gaft placed in a tree to nourish and support it. It unites and becomes one with the tree, but the gaft determines the kind of fruit. Also condition of the whole tree is changed from its very roots. The gaft impedes the circulation if the sap for a time, but the tree is made more fruitful and is enriched in every way.

The true word changes the condition of the mind by enriching and making fruitful in right thoughts and desires. If we object to it we are irritated, or as some call it, "stirred up," but that is only a good sign.

When one who conscientiously believes in evil, and that there is a God who not only permits but ordains evil, is told that as God is only Good there cannot be any evil, he at once says, "That is utter nonsense," and feels indignant that he is listening to such talk. To him there is no reasoning or philosophy in it, for can he not see all about him evidences of evil?

Still he is not able to rid himself of the new idea, and in some mysterious way the old beliefs seems to have lost its firm hold of his mind. He ponders upon this new idea, turning it over and over in his mind, feeling anything but free or happy. It has taken such a hold that it will not leave him, and the more that he combats it the closer it clings. He is in a miserable state, for he does not quite believe anything now.

He has borne the burden of evil and sin so long that he does not know how to lay it down. It has been his constant companion and to give it up seems like a great loss. Truth always "shineth in darkness and the darkness comprehendeth it not."

The darkness of his mortal beliefs will not yet allow him to see the truth. But the true word will and must work in the mind. No word of truth is ever lost. So, while he cannot get rid of these words of truth that make him uncomfortable, he concludes that if he can get more truth he may feel better.

Now there is no use in pretending that the very next words such an one hears fill him with joy, light breaking suddenly over him to illuminate him with understanding, for such is not the case *except very rarely*.

The little plant just putting its head above ground does not at once shoot up into a bush or tree, but must have tender care, sun, and rain to make it grow. The word of truth wants the nurture of faith and use in order to blossom or bring forth fruit.

We sometimes are obliged to work in order to obtain faith that the word is true. There are many Thomas's in the world, and such must work to see the fruit of the word before they fully accept it. This kind seldom go back when a step is once taken. They are the plodding ones but the sure ones even if they never have the brilliant, illumined experiences others tell of.

Ecstasies are transient, and not often productive of valuable help to the word; not only that, but they are not always from the Spirit, they are often induced by imagination. We must "try the spirits," as John said, to see "whether they are of God."

The quickest way out of any dilemma, indecision, or trouble, is to follow the advice of Carlyle in a like case. It was curt but to the point. "Work," he said, and Goethe said, "Do the duty that lieth nearest thee." In this lies the deepest wisdom, for not only is it a panacea for every ill, but only through doing, through work, comes more light.

So if the student who hears that "all is good" will stop pondering and combating and look for good in everybody and everything, he will surely see it, and if we will take care to do only good to all, his understanding will shine for the more quickly.

If we fall into the line of truth we shall not show forth the change it makes, except perhaps by a new radiance of countenance, but like floating down stream with the current, it will be very easy and pleasant. As the boat would go of itself without help from us, so truth will work of itself if we are passive, and its working will give us new hopes, new aims, new desires, thus making chemicalization only a pleasure.

The one who is made uncomfortable by the first words of truth but concludes he needs more, next hears that he must for even if he sees someone cruelly treated there is no evil there; no reality in the seeming; the seeming is not true. To be told this makes him very angry as he is quite sure he knows what he sees.

If he understood thought he would know that anger is a sign of force, and that force should be directed to the one who is cruel (seemingly) with the thought that no one *can be* cruel, no one can do any harm to anyone in this universe where only Good reigns. He should say, with the vehemence that anger gives, that the seemingly cruel one is good in Soul. That only good can result from his acts for evil is powerless.

It is this way of sending out helpful thoughts over the world that cleanses the world-self and throws out the errors or false ways, to make way for truth to work effectively.

He must use this anger in working for the world, and not allow it to master him as of old.

Spirit shows a better way, a way to harness all characteristics to the service of the good, and thus teaches how to be rid of what are called evil tendencies. Denial uncovers all that was hid that we may dispose of all in the best way.

This is to "let the earth bring forth"-or manifest-show forth, all that is within, for as we declare spiritual truth-the only reality-the earthly ways are pushed into view to be dealt with according to law-made nothing.

We train our thoughts into the true channel by declaring persistently that all is Spirit and that material things are nothing at all-only an appearance-and that the Spirit if us is the only reality, no matter how stirred up we feel, or how untrue it sounds.

We are determined to follow the rules given us, that are said to bring the happiest results; that are promised to bring neighbor or friend, for healing is but the bringing forth the real Self-the Spirit that cannot be sick or need healing.

The only work is to make the true self shine forth, and we deal with the one who comes to us for help as we train ourselves.

What has been called "a patient" is simply one who is imprisoned by a certain mode of thought; is in chains and has come to one who is wiser than himself to have the chains knocked off that the airs of freedom may blow over him.

Only truth sets free, so our work is to declare that he is Spirit only and never was anything else,-never was born of flesh as his mortal thought told him, - and to deny that he or she can  be deceived into believing anything concerning flesh or material ways, or be influenced by the beliefs of other people, because he is like Spirit the creator in all things.

We keep firmly to our argument, no matter what signs he shows forth of being stirred by it. If truth caused the stir, the change, in his mind, is truth not powerful enough to quell it and make calm and peaceful?

Surely it is; so we keep on giving words of truth, at the same time quieting all fear by saying in a soothing, calming, gentle way (mentally), "You have nothing to fear, for you are Spirit, and Spirit cannot fear anything at all."

Every mother knows how she catches her little child up in her arms when it has fallen and hurt itself, saying, "There, there, baby is all right, nothing shall hurt you, mother will take care of her little one," and when the mother has kissed the spot and spoken in the caressing, soothing tone of voice, the child runs to its play again.

This is what all the grown up children need to quiet their fears that cause all the "chemicalization."

The Spirit is just as tender as a loving mother and takes us in its everlasting, infinite arms, soothing and healing us through right words. We know this and must tell the good news to the patient, who wants just this news from a far country to make him joyous and glad.

Many a person will get well if simply told silently that there is nothing to fear, for fear is the principal cause of sickness in the world, and in addressing one who believes in sickness, according to the rule or formula, this fear is aroused by mention being made of the sin or sins he has believed he was specially guilty of.

All believe that they have offended God in some way and fear the penalty, so that the declaration, "there is no sin," or, "you cannot sin, suffer for sin, nor fear sin"- which simply means the same as the beautiful words of Jesus, "thy sins be forgiven thee," will stir the mind, or startle it, and this change the body shows as quickly as the register of an electric bell when the button is pressed.

It is the mind that is to be impressed or treated, and the body is the reporting sheet that tells what we have accomplished, so when the patient comes to us saying she is worse, is feverish, restless, or in pain, or sick all over, these are only symptoms of the mental condition.

We know that the true words have taken hold of the mind, as a dose of mandrake would take hold of the body. Everyone used to believe that after the bitter herb had stirred the liver to cast out all that made the blood acid or impure the body would be well, and that made people patiently bear all the sick, bad feelings. They looked forward to the renewed, purified condition to come.

Truth does just that to the mind; casts out the errors that are acid to it, leaving it pure and wholesome, so we know this sickness to be good, only a sign of the healthy thoughts coming forth- a casting out of wrong beliefs.

Spirit, truth, cleanses mortal mind; purifies, pushes out all error; takes down the cobwebs of wrong belief.

Each true, cleansing thought pushes out some wrong one which is a portion of the rubbish clogging the mind, and as it goes, the body reports the change. If we struggle to hold the error, the body is shaken and shows pain, depression, or sickness, as we call it.

These are in reality but signs that the Good is doing its work, is trying to restore the balance to mind; that Spirit is trying to assert its supremacy, its rightful mastery.

This is all very like the process of cleaning house. Do we not throw aside all unnecessary things cumbering the rooms from attic to cellar, remove all dust and smoke from the walls, and make the windows bright and clear for the light to shine through?

This material process can be made very disagreeable and uncomfortable by groaning over every trifle connected with it. Determining at the start that it is a terrible ordeal to go through, fearing that this or that will not be done in the right way and fretting generally. Is not that a stirring up of the whole household?

But there is no need of it, for it can be and is done by

plenty of people in an orderly, methodical, quiet manner, sothat the inmates of the house scarcely know that it is being done at all.

There is nothing like system, and the mind is systematic if not interfered with by error, receiving truth as the plant takes water, gratefully and gladly, springing forth into fruitage or blossoming at exactly the right moment.

The case of asthma we have been describing is no exception to the majority of cases in showing the signs of what is going on within. We are not frightened when she is frightened. We do not notice if she is uncomfortable. Why should we? Truth is cleansing, renovating. We feel the peace of truth while she complains of the disturbance of error. She had expected to get well right away, of course. This is the right thing to expect, without any bad feeling. But the body registers the mind. By extra sickness she showed confusion of mind. If the family are disturbed also, the whole of them blame the science for making her uncomfortable.-People always attribute to the science all the mortal mind's showing forth of error. Very probably our friend has confidence enough in our knowledge of science to believe that we can help her. We inspire confidence by the truth we are thinking. Did you ever see snow cleared from a railroad track? See the snow pushed to right and left leaving the track clear and smooth? Well, science is doing that with all who are spoken to in truth, but who feel unconscious opposition. Truth pushes all except true thought out of mind, and each thought affects the body. Tell every body that when these feelings are gone they will be better than they ever were before, because their health will be established upon the firm basis of the health that is God. Tell sick people some things audibly in order to give them greater confidence in what is being done.

Tell them mentally that there is nothing to fear from anywhere or anybody. Confusion and discord in the race or in the past among ancestors, have no power to disturb in any way.

Confusion and discord in friends cannot affect in the least. There is nothing to fear at all. There is no inharmony of any kind from any direction that can disturb or make afraid. Spirit is peace. There is no discord or inharmony within the self mind that makes fear. There is no discord or inharmony in the speaker's mind that can affect to bring confusion. Say quite firmly, "I myself, send you only courage and fearlessness, for I trust in Spirit, and Spirit knows peace. I am peace."

Say within your own mind softly and graciously, "God is your life, it cannot be threatened with death, nor fear death, nor yield to death at all. God is your health; it cannot be threatened with sickness, nor fear sickness, nor yield to sickness ever. God is your strength; it cannot be threatened with weakness, nor fear weakness, nor yield to weakness ever.

"God is your peace; it cannot be threatened with discord or inharmony, nor fear discord or inharmony, nor yield to discord or inharmony ever. God is your peace, your perfect peace.

"You trust in God. You are perfectly sound and well in every part. You are alive with the life of Spirit; you are strong with the strength of Spirit; you are bold with the boldness of Spirit; you trust in God."

At night give the same treatment –absently.

Any acute attack is chemicalization, for it shows that some word of truth has struck hard upon some error of thought, and is pushing it out of the mind. For such we must use denial, but in a negative and indifferent manner. If one has any sudden illness in your presence it shows that two kinds of thoughts have collided. When we can see that fear is the cause of sickness we deny a great deal, speaking coolly and firmly.

"Fever or inflammation needs cold, indifferent, mental speaking in denial, for the thoughts we send must take the place of the cooling, quieting drinks and applications the mortal mind uses in medication. One who has fainted must be spoken to rapidly and vigorously to rouse quick action of his mind. Deny fear and affirm spiritual joy and safety. Any low, cold, lifeless condition needs warm, stirring affirmations. This is all condition of human life reducible to mind and manageable by mind. To understand mind is the highest of all attainment.

# NOTES

# NOTES

CHAPTER XI.

## Fifth Power of Law.-Foolishness and Ignorance Dispelled.

When we first hear that according to our thoughts is our bodily condition, we feel as f we might always be well. If that is true, for we have no desire to have any but good and true thoughts.

But when we try to use the Truth by directing our thoughts to another, and that other does not at once get well, the temptation comes to try some material process to help more quickly than our thoughts seem to do.

If we have really accepted the teachings of the new old doctrine, that God's presence is all about us and able and willing to save to the uttermost, all who come to Him, and that He loves all His children exactly the same, we know that our whole dependence is upon Him; that in Him is the only real health, so we reason with ourselves to make assurance doubly sure, for a perfect conviction that this being true we have nothing to do but trust; we determine to feel quite sure that nothing can come to us to do that we are not perfectly capable of doing.

If our friend does not get well and happy by our thoughts as we expect, the fault is in our own way of thinking, for of course it is easily understood that every thought we send out is tinged with our own quality of mind, or the conscious or unconscious ideas we hold-prejudices if we have any-for

"Hide in your heart a bitter thought,
Still it has power to blight,"

is law as well as poetry.

All our thoughts are carried to our friends who are complaining, and they may take more of our errors and more readily than they take the truth if they choose. We should be entirely lost too all mortal thoughts, absorbed in the divine presence and the words we are speaking, but if we have not yet become thoroughly one with Truth it may an effort or strain to keep mortal thoughts away and concentrate all our power upon the work of right thinking. If this is so our feeble friends feel the tension of our mind are not swiftly benefited by us. If we are anxious they feel this very quickly, for they are very susceptible to any influence. They are looking to us for help with all their heart, and their mind is alert with expectancy. This "expectant attention" as it has been called, has put them into a passive condition, has made their mind blank like a clean slate, and we write upon it whatever we think and feel.

We must be careful what thoughts we write upon the state of mind and how they are colored with emotions. Thoughts have been compared to the rainbow, each kind of a color, as, love is red, wisdom yellow, truth blue, purity white. Then envy, jealousy and all kindred thoughts must be symbolized by dark colors, or black.

A simple-hearted, child-like trust in God, the kind and loving father so near, will do more to help the patient than any exertion of ours.

We heard of one who healed all who came to him by saying and holding firmly the words, "God is Supreme."

If God is Supreme power, health, strength, peace, and all

contrary conditions must fall away from His presence, which is in all places. When we believe this so strongly that we know it perfectly, all disease must fall away from the fire of such healing, loving, thoughts.

Until we can realize such truth in every fiber of our mind we must keep to the rule. But the rule is only to train the mind to reach realization or understanding of the highest conception of truth. There is only God in the universe. This is the highest truth. All mortality with its sin, sickness, and death, must flee before this truth when we fully realize it, as dew before the sun or darkness before light.

To realize a truth is to do more than to believe, even more than to know it. It is to prove that we know it, by showing forth in our acts that we do so, by demonstrating to others the knowledge that we have; "knowledge is power." If we truly know that God is all, and that all "our help cometh from the Lord," our every act, word thought and look will prove it. How? By loud talk of our power and vain glory in our speech, proclaiming our birthright?

Not at all. "The fruit of the spirit is peace, gentleness, love, meekness and temperance." "If we live in the spirit let us also *walk* in the spirit."

We show forth exactly what we think, for we cannot help doing so, and it is proved and felt by others through our silent influence.

If we in any degree realize, or even believe in the presence of God as a creative power, we do not give or advocate any material processes for healing or reforming. We Hold steadily to the words of Truth, confident of their working efficiency.

If we do not feel entire confidence in our own capability to use the words of truth to bring the best results, we must pray till we do trust.

Now true prayer is thankfulness to the Friend who never faileth, that He is giving us just the blessing we desire, and trust that it is sure to become manifest, so we pray, "Father I thank thee that this thy child is perfectly well and whole as thou didst create him, and now thou wilt prove it."

This gives us the needed calmness to pray effectually, assured of perfect safety in the presence of God.

We must never feel that we ourselves are more anxious to cure a neighbor than to have someone else do so, for this is ambition which is not a healing thought to convey to any one by any means.

We can be very sure of one thing, viz., that truth itself unadulterated by mortal thought will cure anything. All we need do is to cleanse our thoughts by denial and "watch and pray" to keep our mind clear, pure and true.

Just as our thoughts and words carry our mental condition, so do writings. We read a book and feel depressed, or chilled, or as if we were friendless and alone in the world, hopeless and desolate. It is from the mental condition of the writer.

Of course this signifies that we are to deny that we can be affected at all by any qualities of mind. Then when we take up any kind of a book it cannot disturb us.

To admit that we can be affected by anybody or anything is acknowledging another power besides God.

If a writer or speaker, or one who converses with us, or is even in our vicinity , has a cruel or vindictive habit of thinking, or unconsciously has this state of mind, he will give us a feeling of despair if we do not understand the defense of Spirit.

A sordid mind will cause a feeling as if we were smothered or could not breathe. A coarse, low state of mind near us or in books will give us nausea. A selfish person will cause cancer in himself or others. One with false ideas will take away from others the powers of judgment. It is what we are in habit and belief that goes out and strikes others with whom we come in contact, not so much what we say. A father may talk with a man and get an influence from him which he will carry to his child, and it will develop into diphtheria or scarlet fever. Thought is the contagion and epidemic, instead of bacteria. "Guard well thy thoughts." Contagious thoughts and bodily sickness are all mortal ways of thinking and doing, and to be above all such we must be acquainted with the ways and laws of Spirit. Then our position is unalterable by transactions of any kind; is unassaible, for "none of these things move me," though then thousand mortal minds were leagued to decree destruction. We are folded round with safety by the ever-living, powerful presence of God. It is an impenetrable armor.

Spirit and matter *cannot* mingle, cannot take cognizance of each other, so if we are encased in Spirit, no thoughts of matter can penetrate the armor. They are arrows that will rebound to those who sent them, to work upon themselves their mission.

It is best to read only what tells of sweetness, purity,

happiness, health, love and tenderness, whatever is uplifting and makes us desire to be good and true. Whatever writing or reading tells of aught else, not only profiteth nothing but brings the suffering and trouble it describes, all tending to the end of physical life, for all belief in evil carries suffering with it.

It is extremely unwise to talk of these conditions of our friends, or to say they are not getting alone well, or to speak of their past troubles. The past of self and others must be ignored until actually forgotten. All we have to do with is the present, and if we attend to our duties our hands are full enough.

We heard of a lady who described to a friend a past illness in a very graphic manner, and the result was a recurrence of the same condition. Why will we not learn by the experience of others?

We read that, "civilization is profited by the experience of others" and why should not spiritualization come by the same process?

While we speak of the slowness of a mind to respond to true words it may be just ready to show forth perfect health. That moment may be just what is called in physical sickness, "the crisis," the turning point to recovery. At that moment we ought to be thinking our best of him. One who knows the law of Truth of Spirit, knows that all we see, all we experience, are but signs that health is striving to show forth, to burst the bonds of mortal ways and show how glorious all things really are.

There is no sign of anything but good in Spirit. No matter what occurs to us or what is said, no matter how hard it at first seems, we must quickly detect the good to come from it. For instance, one we considered a friend judges us unjustly; at first it seems very hard to be so keenly disappointed in one we valued, but if we say, "None of these things move me, I am Spirit and that is a mortal transaction," presently we find that we have been freed from a so-called friendship, which would have proved a yoke about our necks. We see the mortal as it shows forth in time to strike the fetters off even before they are fully forged. There is nothing comparable to freedom, and one who would in the least hamper ours is not a friend.

Spirit leads and guides us if we let It, and we need no mortal dictation. The gentle Spirit will see that we have none. All that is mortal must expose itself by using mortal language and actions, for in the presence of Spirit the mortal is never content. It chemicalizes or ferments, showing its hydra heads unmistakably.

Do we not desire to be freed from such, no matter at what cost in the seeming? The Spirit is our Hercules to slay it for us. We can afford to be gentle and gracious, looking past mortality's ways to the perfect child of God who must come forth through such rough, thorny ways if he has not chosen the meek and lowly way in which the first living word of Truth walked.

Spirit takes care of its own, and mortal ways *must* stand aside.

Error is its own destruction or annihilation, and we need not have even a passing wish for anyone to ne punished for the greatest or the least error. The punishment, as we call it, is so sure to come, according to law, that we may stand with bated breath to see the working of law.

Suppose we are persecuted for truth's sake, or our words and actions falsified and misrepresented. If we remember that these are mortal ways only, and say the words of Jesus, "Glorify Thou me with Thine own self," the Spirit will work for us an exceeding weight of glory.

Spirit is true, is sure, and we can safely rest in It. Suppose we *are* forsaken of all others? Spirit says, "I will never leave thee nor forsake thee," and is not "God able of these stones to raise up children" for our companions and friends?

Anyone who has believed in signs must now declare everything a sign of good. The things that we used to call signs of death we now call signs of the end of mortal ways. Having visions we must be sure to declare them signs of great good to come. To see what seems to be a skeleton is a sign that all fleshly ways are gone from the person it resembles. If we see before us a face with deathlike hue we must say that mortal ways are dead to that person, and he is awake to righteousness (right thought).

A lady saw before her ghastly face with a hole in the temple. It simply meant that her thought had penetrated his mind and he was dead to old ways of thinking. If one hears the imaginary tolling of a bell, it means that old ways are being rung out; they are dead. We must turn the tolling into petals of joy at the new birth-of Spirit.

If a dog howls, that great bugbear of superstition, say he is speaking for the end of some wrong. It is the animal instinct to howl and cry when it feels that it is losing its hold upon man. Yet it is good to be free from all animality.

If we see a light over us we may be sure that we are

guided and it must fill us with trust, beautiful trust.

Symbols are not signs of spiritual growth, but if we see them we must interpret them wisely. All is for good for life, health and happiness. There is nothing else in reality, and we have no right to think of any other condition. Even our dreams should be scientific, all for good. When we feel the indication of some form of so-called sickness creeping over us we must say, "This is fear leaving me because I am filled with courage. Every breath I draw is from God. God is courage is itself." Or say, "This is but a sign of present health driving out any appearance to the contrary."

All these old ways are but ways of ignorance and foolishness. One of the greatest teachers of the world found out that ignorance was the cause of all misery among men.

Now that we know Truth is it not foolish to still cling to ignorance? Freedom from ignorance and foolishness is what we all want, and Truth is the only power that will make us free. We must cling to It as the drowning man clings to whatever comes in his way, with all the strength and of desperation.

And we must deny that ignorance and foolishness can have any power at all over us. Anxiety and fear, like all mortal mind tendencies, are good servants but bad masters, and we must control them by banishment from the mind, to give place to hope and courage and fearlessness. If we declare that we are filled with courage and fearlessness and adhere to it, fear must and will go.

When a mind with its body chemicalizes, we know that we have touched upon the special sin that it believe it has inherited or is addicted to. The cause of all sickness is sin, so by denying sin or erasing it from the mind sickness disappears. If we are jealous, envious, selfish, or revengeful, we cannot be well until we are rid of either or all of these traits.

People who are helped by science treatments often wonder why they do not remain well while their helper is absent from them. Simply because they have work to do themselves, and must learn to control their own thoughts, their own sins, as they are called. No physician warrants a cure permanently, especially if the patient breaks physical law continually. Physical performances symbolize mental experiences, and neither can a metaphysician pretend to warrant a cure if the mind will go on thinking wrongly and clinging to sins. A metaphysician might be kept thinking for us by the year, as physicians are sometimes employed, but there would yet be thoughts that each mind should think independently. Some are changed by a few thoughts, but they are those who willingly give up all wrong tendencies. All these causes may be unconscious to the person.

Sometimes, if we fail to help our friends by the "form of sound words"- the rule of mind-and are not spiritually advanced enough to realize that God is indeed all there is and there can be nothing else in all the universe, we may be able to realize that Jesus Christ is as near to us as he was to any one when on earth, and that he is as loving, tender and ready to heal as then, and will do so if we ask him.

Then we can say to those near us who need our words, "Through Christ the Truth you are healed." If we are close to the Christ Spirit He will do the healing for us.

When we realize that God is truly all there is, we are very

likely to have some word that expresses God take a firm hold on our mind, and by keeping it in mind it will do the healing. "God is Life." We can say this over and over till the room is alive with lif;' the patient will feel revived and feel new life stirring all through him. If we say *"love"* over and over in mind it will steal softly over the atmosphere and heal; or the word "peace." We can say, "All is Spirit" until we do not see the body of flesh at all, only the perfect spiritual creation in the image and likeness of God.

Being healed is simply being taught about God, just as if were children. Did we not always feel better after hearing about God from mother or teacher or any one who told us how good, loving and tender God was; that He was everywhere and would never leave us; would always take care of us, fold us in his arms, and did not this make us feel happy? It was a healing teaching when were indeed children, and so it is now. Healing is only teaching about God.

After a stirring up of the physical mane he, of course, is weak, just as one would be who had carried a heavy burden for a long time. The mortal mind has borne the burden of error for a long time, and when it has been away by denial, a vacuum is left which shows out as weakness of body. It is said that "nature abhors a vacuum." To Spirit there is no vacuum, for it fills all space. Spirit is mind, then if mind is cleansed from error, Spirit has its rightful sway.

When anyone is feeble, weak, exhausted, languid or tired, he is in the condition to receive a particular idea whether we have given other ideas to him or not. Whether we have ever spoken one word of Truth to him or not, he has had it from some source, and it has chemicalized him, leaving him weak; so he needs a special word. The alkali of Truth has disturbed and destroyed the error, and this is the result: the new base that is just right to receive strong, true words, and will make a strong, healthy mind and body.

This weak condition shows how ignorant of Truth our friend was, and proves that he believed in the law of matter-or nature, as it is called-and that, if he disobeyed such law he must be sick or get old and die.

Such belief is extreme of foolishness, for flesh that "profieth nothing" has no laws. Is it not foolish to believe that the man that God made to have "dominion over the earth" could be subject to earth laws, or that there could be any such laws?

Is not man foolish to refuse his birthright as God's child; foolish to ignore the presence of Spirit from which he might draw infinite health, strength and wisdom continually?

To be wise is to be in a perfect condition, for the without must be as the within. They who are wise do not speak of disease or pain or weakness or trouble, because they know that these are not evidences of truth, but of false thoughts; foolish and ignorant beliefs. The wise tell only the truth at all times, so they show out Truth and their very bodies become spiritualized, sound, firm, hardy and enduring.

They breathe Spirit and lean upon Spirit for strength and vigor, and know that they need only God to support and sustain life. They give no attention to heat or cold, to food or drink, to money or friends, but seek first the kingdom off God, and all these things are added.

They speak the truth about strength, vigor and courage, no matter what appears; no matter how much weakness and feebleness seem to be true, for they know that these are but proof that strength and vigor are within, pushing out the untrue, unreal condition.

Weakness and feebleness are evidences of ignorance and foolishness, so when we see anybody in that condition we must deny ignorance and foolishness, saying, "You are not weak or feeble, you are not tired or exhausted or languid. I refuse to acknowledge that you are suffering the consequences of past or present foolishness and ignorance of our parents, or of the whole race-mind; you are not suffering the consequences of foolishness and ignorance of the people around you; you are not suffering the consequences of your own foolishness and ignorance; you are not suffering for my foolishness and ignorance, for I am not foolish and ignorant at all.

"God is your life; you cannot be threatened with death, nor fear death, nor yield to death.

"God is your health; you cannot be threatened with disease or sickness, nor fear disease or sickness, nor yield to disease or sickness ever.

"God is your strength; you cannot be threatened with weakness, nor fear weakness, nor yield to weakness at all.

"God is your peace; you cannot be threatened with discord or inharmony, nor fear discord or inharmony, nor yield to discord or inharmony ever. You are perfectly sound and well in every part.

"You are alive with the life of the Spirit; you are bold with the boldness of Spirit; you are strong with the strength of the Spirit.

"You trust in God."

"You are live and strong and vigorous and hardy; energetic and bold and sound and well-*and you know it.*"

It is reasonable to think that if it makes a great difference to our friends what we are thinking about, that a warming, invigorating manner of thinking about their wonderful strength, life, energy and joyousness, will make them feel the opposite of feeble and exhausted. If everybody would purposefully in a joyous and buoyant manner it would lift the despair and weariness of the world. It is possible to think in this way, and as so many are now practicing it, we may expect the new heaven and the new earth.

# NOTES

NOTES

CHAPTER XII.

## The Sixth Power of Law is The Triumph of Truth, or Perfect Health.

We may be inclined to think that when one whom we have been sending strong truth in the silence of our mind, says he or she is well, there is nothing for us to do; but this is not so.

There is never a time when it is not right and best to speak some true words. Principle never ceases. There never is a time when people are not bettered by a true thought, no matter how well they may be. We must be experts in the realm of thought, just as necessarily as a mechanic must be an expert in the realm of mechanics. Would he become so without practice, steady and persistent, in studying and working upon machines? He must study the mechanism in all its details, must know exactly the bearing of one part upon another, before he can make it work perfectly, or explain all about it to other people.

Thoughts are things, and we must practice handling, controlling and directing them, for the good of the world, and unwearingly, until we are so alive with wisdom that we not only know just what to say to each person, just the word to help him best, just what thought to send, but our very presence is sufficient to banish pain, trouble, disease, and all mortal conditions, from all whom come near us.

We are like what we study, or like those with whom we associate, and if we study God, or causing power, we also have the same power. If we study Mind we know how to deal with mind and all its ways. If we study Spirit, live close to Spirit we become so at one with It, so imbued or permeated with It that we radiate a spiritual influence that can be plainly felt by all who enter our presence. There is an unmistakable, perceptible influence in a spiritual presence, that every one can feel, and this heals and blesses. This state is called understanding of God, or realization of Truth.

Now some people seem to think that when God is understood, there is no more work to be done, none necessary, no necessity for demonstration of what we are. Was it so easy to reach this height of thought that God and man are one, are inseparable, that we can rest forever from proving the assertion? Can we remain in that position without effort? Is there any other proof of our words except demonstration in our life that we know whereof we speak?

If all people had reached the plane of spiritual understanding possibly we could rest from our labors, but while one remains in ignorance, we have a work to do like our Creator: the work of creating, or bringing forth the true creation that is within every child of God.

These children of God in the world look sharply and closely for demonstration of every word we speak, and they are right, for Jesus Christ said, "If I do not the works of My Father believe me not." If we say, "I and my Father are one," people look to see god-like works in thought, word, and deed. If we say, "I am the expression of Spirit that is God; I am one with Spirit, inseparable from it," people look to see proof of our words in our acts, our works. Job said, "doth not the ear try words?"

There is no one living who has not enough recognition

of the pure life of Spirit to know when practice is consistent with profession. We have had words and repetitions of words all through the centuries, that were beautiful in themselves but were made of no avail, empty and vain, because the life, the works, of the one whose lips uttered them did not coincide with them, did not demonstrate that he indeed knew them to be true.

What is the use of giving a child the rule in mathematics, unless we show him how to use it in working out problems, show him the demonstration of its being true, and of use to him?

What is the use of giving to the world the principle of life and health and happiness, unless we show by our works that we know whereof we speak?

All students watch and scrutinize the life of a great teacher of ethics to see if there is one single discrepancy to be found. Words are empty and vain, worse than "sounding brass and tinkling cymbals," unless accompanied by works. No matter what talent, what ability, what eloquence, what persuasion a man has, it all counts for nothing, if he show not forth works in accord with his words.

Jesus Christ laid great stress upon works all through his teaching. He said, "The Father doeth the works," "My Father worketh hitherto and I work." Paul said, "God works through you to will and to do."

If the light in a lighthouse were continually kept burning, but was hidden by curtains at the windows, would any mariner be guided by its beams safely into port?

We have been told to "let our light shine that we

may glorify the Father in heaven." If we simply say we have the light, are one with it, is that shedding the beams upon the world, proving that we shine? No more than telling the mariner that the light burns, after he has gone out of the proper course.

If we do no works we hide our light under a bushel, and not only that, but we shall lose consciousness that we are the light.

While we are obliged to learn by symbols, the so-called laws of physics are used as symbols of metaphysics. A law of physics is that if we do not use any part of the body we are sure to lose the use of it; so if we do not use any faculty of mind we must lose the power to use it.

Is not this a shadow of the real law, for has not man had the spiritual faculty lying dormant all these ages, because he did not use it? Would it not again become dormant if not used, and is there any way to prove even to ourselves its use except through works? All else is mere sentiment. Feeling is all right when wedded to its complement, the word of truth, for it then produces evidence of doing something. The law is to have something being done.

Not one will deny that God expresses himself; must express himself. If that expression is not demonstration, work, what can we call it?

When the rose ceases to give forth fragrance does it now at once begin to wither, and lose its leaves, till nothing is left but the unsightly, bare calyx? Our fragrance is produced by work, within self and for others. When this ceases there is no sweet, benign, hallowing influence emanating from our presence. It is continual giving, giving forth of what we are, that causes us to inhale more and more of the spirit of love, and in turn exhale it, proving that we have kept the commands of Spirit, and that the Father has "taken up his abode in us."

In material things, springs supplied from surface water dry up when they are exposed to the hot summer sun, but those that are supplied from the depths are constantly giving and constantly receiving. Streams that are constantly giving are constantly receiving. The blood in the human body is ceaselessly shifting from one part to the other, so that every part of the body is visited by every drop of blood. Thus we see that life is motion, and stagnation of water or blood breeds disease and death.

The law of God is, Give forth and you shall be supplied, replenished.

Some people think that they must wait for thorough understanding of Principle before they can do any satisfactory work. This is an error. We must use what we do know in order to know more.

What would happen to a reservoir if it never gave forth its contents, and yet the water continually ran into it? If would overflow and cause destruction in all directions.

We are reservoirs of understanding, and the supply must go forth from us as fast as we receive it, in order to keep it strong and clear. It strengthens us in knowledge to use our knowledge for others.

It has been said that "we study to know, and know to understand." We should say, we study to work, and we work in order to understand.

A stopped up current becomes muddy, and if we do not give forth as we receive, we shall not show forth our clearness in understanding. Can we not see that Spirit does not do the work for us with no response on our part? For the same Spirit has been right here always and yet we have not seen the works.

We have our part to perform else we are automatons. God works through us to will; then ours must be the will to do. The opportunity and supply will follow.

To think right thoughts is to think only good thoughts; thus keeping in the current of the good has not been done automatically as all can testify.

It is natural for the regenerated mind, the one who is born again of Spirit, to desire to help others; to do something for them that they may know the new birth. This is an excellent sign, for anyone who earnestly desires to have others helped is coming out of his shell of selfishness. Sickness always makes us selfish, because we think constantly of our feelings and wishes.

When we are giving the healing words of truth to any one, and he tells us how grateful he is for benefit received, speaks of wanting others to know about the wonderful law and be helped, then is the time to give the sixth portion of the law, or sixth word of the spiritual doctrine.

It is the highest spiritual word,-all affirmation,-and the last statement of the rule of health. This rule embraces just six statements, and the six may all be compassed by one word when we thoroughly understand both rule and doctrine of Spirit.

When we know perfectly that there is but one health

in all universe and that is God, and that it is everywhere to the total exclusion of disease, then all we need say to the sick is, "health." That one word means to us all there is of rules; all there is of law. For to say or hold in the mind that as God is health itself, the patient is health also, is to hold the full statement of the rule of truth, for if all is health this implies or embraces the denial of disease and sickness. It is both denial and affirmation.

To say "God is all," excludes all idea of sickness, trouble, or disease, for we all know that such things can not be in the presence of God-or life, or love, or truth, or Spirit, when wholly realized; for all either one means, will cure anything, and is sufficient to use, because it embraces the entire six statements. But to use one word understandingly we must be above all belief in mortal conditions and truly see only Spirit. While we recognize any of the complaints of sickness as existing, we must deny them.

If we are working by rule, and one who has received our thoughts comes saying he is cured, and wants others to be cured also, we give the sixth scientific word of Spirit to nature; or if any one should say such things the first time we saw him, or the second, or third, or at any time at all, give this mental affirmation.

This is often the very treatment to give to one who is apparently passing away from earth. It is such a warm, life giving affirmation, that it has brought many back to visible life. It is stirring life. Speaking the word "Life," over and over will so charge the atmosphere of a room, that one lying very low can be brought back by it.

If we wish to be a power in the world for good, we must cling to the good only; see only good; hear only good; know only good; think only good. Then we shall be strong and steadfast and have good judgment to know always just what word to say to each person we meet.

Sometimes a quick, firm, strong, "No!" is all that is needed, especially if the person is inclined to recount all his troubles or ailments. This rehearsal needs cutting off, nipping in the bud by a stern "No!" (mental of course.)

We must never show impatience at the telling of ailments or symptoms, as they are very real to our friends, and the quickest and best way to make them unreal to them, is by silent teaching. All silent treatment is teaching. But if this does not answer, and one desires to repeat what he has once told about himself, we must tell him gently that it is better not to say anymore about suffering as it will be gone sooner if not talked of.

We should hardly ever tell anyone aloud, that he is well, or not sick, for it generally irritates and will undo the work we have done in the silence.

We should not talk metaphysics to people unless they invite the conversation, never force the subject upon any one, anywhere.

It is well to hold continually in mind, "I am governed by the law of God and cannot sin, suffer for sin, nor fear sin, sickness or death."

The words we hold in mind make the quality we radiate about us, so if we hold error we scatter error abroad lime miasma. If we hold truth we are like sunshine, and warm and vivify and comfort all who come near us. Not only that, but we are guarded from the false ideas of people about us, and guard others also.

These false ideas are like pollen and reproduce their own kind upon whomsoever they alight. They cause all manner of disturbance if we are not guarded.

But one who knows that he is encompassed by only good, folded around by safety, enveloped by Spirit, is guarded, protected, safe indeed.

If one feels sickness at the stomach, very likely a sensual minded person is near, and he must refuse the idea that mortal mind can affect him at all, because he is Spirit and housed in Spirit, wherein is complete safety. A sensual person is likely himself to be troubled with nausea-according to be the natural state.

Sarcasm in one will cause a seemingly unfounded fear to spring up in the mind of some one near, or in his own mind.

Anger will cause headache in self or one near by. Frivolous minds cause a feeling of discouragement. Cruel or malicious minds cause unhappiness or depression. Grasping people carry to others a sensation of smothering; even their own children will gasp for breath. Is there then nothing to demonstrate? But while we must demonstrate each true word we utter, or even think, still we must not lay entire stress upon outward demonstration. That is having the letter instead of, or more than, the spirit.

Remember that no false idea can at all move one whose mind is strayed on God. One who knows for a certainty that Spirit is power, ever present protection against all that is mortal is not only safe himself, but he can change all error in others by thinking only true thoughts toward them, which will bring them into the current of the presence of Spirit-God-and this stream will, must, cleanse them of mortal ways, or error.

When we arrive at the highest point of understanding, and know that Spirit is the only power that works, and we simply hold still and let it work its will through us and for us and by us, we are still doing something, for we are doing the very highest thing there is to do. This is the "be still and know that I am God."

We know that our very presence heals, blesses, comforts, and recreates or regenerates, so that no matter how high we are in understanding, the work is still going on; it is being done through and for us.

When we reach this state there is nothing, hard to us anymore. We are above all mortal transactions, and they pass under our visible eye without our being conscious of them. They are truly phantasmagoria and do not disturb us. Nothing can reach us to hurt us anymore.

We are like a great general who looks out over the whole field; we have a broad, extended view, a view of real life and its great issues. We have no eye for dreams. It is as if we were suspended in air and traveling over the earth. If we passed over chasms, cliffs, rugged mountain crags, we should not know it, being so far above them.

We are suspended above all mortal dealings and pains, in the arms of our tender Father-Mother Spirit. It bears us aloft and gives Its angels charge over us lest we dash our foot against a stone. It numbers the hairs of our heads-such is Its loving care. We can nestle in Its arms and lean upon It, as a child nestles close up to its mother, putting its head upon her bosom with the utmost trust in her power, and confidence in its own safety.

The martyrs were witness to this absorption in the God love, for they did not feel the flames that devoured their flesh. They were full of a divine idea, and lost all sense of materiality. This is what anyone can do and no one need to be fanatical about it. We should never lose our common sense no matter how transcendent our feelings.

Jesus Christ was always calm, equable and quiet, and he lived constantly with God. He gave no outward signs of ecstasies, but came from his solitude, his communing with the Father with a quiet, gentle mien, and it is a noticeable fact that mighty works always followed those seasons. It was thus that He gave expression to the influx of spiritual power.

Mortal shouting and making a noise are far from proving that we are spiritual. It shows that we are not retaining our good sense, or that we never had much, and senseless excitement has unbalanced that little.

Spirit has no such methods. "The fruit of the Spirit is peace, gentleness and meekness." The presence of the Spirit is holy and sacred. "Put off thy shoes from off they feet for the place whereon thou standest is holy ground."

Ezekiel fell upon his face, Moses and Elijah covered their faces, when God spoke to them.

We need no bugle notes or clarion cry to proclaim that we are spiritual or that we walk with God; are one with Him, for every look, every tone of the voice, every act, even teach turn of the body, will tell the story for us. We must remember that the descending of the Spirit as gentle and noiseless as the falling of the dew, and will express itself in and through us.

The last proclamation of spiritual law to the natural man can never be made too often, for it induces into manifestation the life that is our birthright.

We have no right to die or even to be translated. Our duty is to live forever; visible, happy, immortal life, here and now.

The mere fleshy body is at our own disposal. It is always changing whether we will or no, but we can make its changes what we choose. Flesh is earth, and God said, "Let man have dominion over all the earth." Then we are masters of this body and cannot only make it what we please, but can lay it down and take it up at will.

But best of all, we can have it spiritualized by thinking only spiritual thoughts.

This treatment tends to the spiritualization of anyone who gives or receives it.

These are words: "Your are the perfect child of the living God, spiritual, harmonies, free, fearless.

"You reflect all the universe of good. From every direction, everywhere, come the words of truth, making you to know how free you are, and making you show forth to all the world that you are free, wise and immortal. You reflect all the best, and only the best.

"You are white with the glory of God shining over you and through you.

"You reflect all the best from the people around you,

and show forth peace, health and wisdom. You reflect all the best from me, and it helps you to know that you are strong and energetic, vigorous and bold and healthy through and through; trusting in God's presence, resting there; knowing that your life is good for it is God; knowing that your health is good for it is God; knowing that your strength is good for it is God; knowing that your peace is good for it is God.

"You are fearless and strong and brave, and able to do all that belongs to you to do, God working through you to will and to do that which ought to be done by you.

"You are alive with the life of the Spirit; you are strong with the strength of the Spirit; you are sound and well in every part.

"You are a living witness of the power of truth to set free into health and strength and living service for the world.

"Let perfect health now be made manifest by you. Let divine love be now expressed through you.

"The Lord keep you and bless you and cause his face to shine upon you."

The consecutive mental statements in the last six chapters have been proved to be the most efficacious formulas in use, and to cover the ground of any sickness or trouble that can possibly be brought to one who desires to heal others. One need not be a declared practitioner of mental science in order to heal. There is work for each one who reads, hears, or learns of the spiritual law, among his or her own family and friends, in a quiet, unobtrusive way. We need not proclaim to others that we are treating them. We need not stop to be asked. It is our bounden duty to speak the word that frees Spirit, to every human being-(mentally).

These treatments have proved their potency, by not only curing thousands, but by lifting the one who uses them to the highest state of realization of the presence of Spirit and its power to heal all our infirmities. This realization in the great desideratum, the goal we all desire to reach, for through it the quickest cures are made; instantaneous healing is done.

The first five truthful affirmations will cure any imaginable condition, if persistently used with an eye single to the power they contain. The last and sixth (as we have said) is for the assurance of health, and for spiritual understanding.

We have given the "form of sound words" that will heal and also train the mind of whoever uses them, but let it be understood that while this formula is successful, any word that comes forcibly to your mind is the one to use. Any mode of expression peculiar to yourself is your own God given talent. It is the state of the positive thinking mind that determines the cure. If the formula does not appeal to the one who addresses, it is not their fault. If the formula does not appeal to you, look it over carefully. The desire to do things in a manner different from other people, should not prevent us from using a formula, or any special method, that has been successful for others.

Not being successful is the sure evidence of not being on the right track, and we had better not let pride or the hope of vain glory prevent us from following the example of successful thinkers and reasoners.

To us it seems the most natural thing to wish to learn from each one who really demonstrates, just how it is done, and then try the same method.

It has been repeatedly said in these lessons, that realization of the presence and power of God, or understanding, is the acme of knowledge and power, and is the goal we all seek, because that is the most potent method of what we call cure or mortal ills.

Let us above all things use and cultivate judgment by the pathway of meekness. There are cases where this formula might not be as helpful as a few soothing words felt by your loving mind like, "There, there; it is all right."

Experience brings good judgment (perhaps intuition is a better term), to know just what words are best adapted to each situation. If we have a true, sure realization of the vivifying, warming, living, and yet soothing, comforting, calming presence of Spirit everywhere, with each living being, we need no words. We—as it were—bathe all surrounding minds in these waters of health, and they show forth health. We *know* that God is all and is health, so surely that we cannot even say, "You are healed," for we are certain there is nothing else beside health.

When we find our own way of thinking—the one that seems to us as if it must heal, that carries all our heart, all our love with it –we have struck our keynote of truth, and the keynote to our healing power.

The following has been found to be very effectual, especially in absent reasonings. Speak to mind as to a little child, telling the story of truth simply, thus:

"You know that God is everywhere, then He is with you

wherever you are. God cannot be sick. Sickness cannot be where He is; cannot enter His presence. Then, as you *are*, in His presence you cannot be sick, sickness cannot come near you. God is health itself. Thus health is all there is anywhere. It is all about you, and through you. You are one with all health; you are an expression of health. You are perfectly whole. You cannot be anything else."

Sometimes you might speak this way" "All is life, everywhere, for God is life itself. Life cannot be interrupted or broken, so you are all life, filled with it, are one with the life that is God. You are full of warm, stirring, reviving life. You are full of vitality. You are all vitality. You are bright and buoyant and lively and happy for you are whole and sound with perfect life."

Every such manner of thinking we use helps self even more than it helps others, for each thought we send out is not only more deeply impressed upon our own mind by the act of sending, but it goes to others and returns with a double blessing. Blessing him who gives as well as him who receives. This is the inevitable law of giving in all respects. It is the casting our bread upon the waters, and we "*shall* find it after many days."

There is a mental and spiritual quality of mind gained through association with God and His law, from speaking continually about Him either in silent reasoning or audible teaching, that has a marked healing, uplifting influence upon all who come into the atmosphere of such a one, but even this is not true realization unless it brings about instantaneous healing of disease and sin.

Realization us the ultimatum of all study, faith and work, and the test of it is *instantaneous healing*.

Thus we can see plainly where we stand, and whether there is any further need for work. Looking upon all the universe of God as perfect, we hereby withdraw all accusations against everybody and everything, and rest in the assurance that as God is all, there never shall any ill come nigh the dwelling place of man forevermore.

# NOTES

# NOTES

## Treatments.

Treating simply for physical conditions but patches up the body, and is no more than magnetism, medication of massage. They all relieve temporarily.

True, lasting healing must be done in the mind. Thoughts of health must be given in place of the thoughts of sickness people have held. In this way we bring forth the health that is really there, or the true mind that is nothing but health because made by God and from His own Substance-Spirit—whole and perfect.

There is in reality no healing done at all. It is only bringing our health, which has it comes forth, pushes away from before it what we call sickness, as the sun drives away fog. Sickness is only foggy, cloudy thoughts enveloping and composing mortal mind.

In beginning to treat we probably have a feeling of dependence which would express itself thus, "All is Spirit around us; we lean upon Spirit. Here in this blessed Spirit is everything we desire. Here is courage for one, strength for another, peace for another. It is an inexhaustible fountain of all things we can wish for or need."

In treating, speak most to each one of the thing he most needs, and the trouble he tells of indicates his need. All we need to know any supposed disease or condition for, is to indicate to us the need of the mind, that we may give the right kind of thoughts.

If a patient is full of fear he needs courage; if

nervousness, he needs peace and calmness. It will touch some minds more to speak of love and comfort than it would to speak of health, although health certainly embraces everything.

The sun is a symbol of Spirit, silent, effective. The sun is everywhere and we cannot get away from it unless we shut ourselves up in some dark place. Spirit is like sunshine and we do not get away from it except by shutting ourselves into the darkness of wrong thoughts.

We have heard of sun baths. We are bathed in Spirit just as the sun bathes the bather. The sun has life, vigor, strength, health, and growth in it. Spirit has a million times more of these, for it is life, vigor, health, strength and growth itself.

The sun is always shining, steady and reliable. If clouds hide it from our view we know that it still shines, and have patience until the clouds are gone.

Spirit is only hidden from our view by our own clouds of error, which we may be rid of by denial.

The command of Jesus to bathe in the pool, was but typical of bathing in the Spirit, the immortal flame of life—the pool of health.

If we speak to a patient (mentally) and cannot find readily right words, speak the name again, and after a moment, again, or until we feel as if her attention were arrested, as if she were really listening.

### Treatment for Weakness

Call name. Listen to what I tell you. You know that God is everywhere present, then He is with you. Pain and sickness, or weakness, cannot come near God for they are impossible in

His presence. Then pain, sickness and weakness cannot come near you, as you are in His presence always.

God is health itself, so there is nothing but perfect health near you. You are one with it, and you are filled with health, strength, peace and rest. You are perfectly whole.

All our words must be repeated until we feel as if people had been filled with them to overflowing.

### For Weakness Without Pain.

Name_____You believe in God and know He is with you always. He is health, strength and rest. Nothing else can be where He is. There is only God. God is all. (Several times.) You have health, vigor, strength, and courage, for God fills you full of them. Spirit is all there is, and is with you and in you, You are whole, now.

### Another For Weakness.

You know that God is Everywhere. The Spirit is all around you. Its arms are about you, resting and refreshing you. You rest in Spirit and are with it. You are covered with peace and rest. You are one with strength and health. You are an expression of strength and health. You are whole.

### Debility

Spirit is all around you like the bright sunshine. You are bathed in it like as in a sun bath. It penetrates every corner and you cannot hide from it. It fills all space. Spirit is health and strength and vigor. You are one with this Spirit, made of It. You are Spirit. Then you are health, strength, vigor, and there is nothing else for you to be. You are perfect and whole, for God made you within himself.

### For A Cold.

Spirit is all—is all around you—it fills you—fills your head so that no cold is there. Spirit fills you and there cannot be two things filling you at the same time. Your head does not burn and ache. It is soothed and healed. (Over and over.)

It is all full of the sweet soothing Spirit. It is like oil to your head and throat. You are healed and soothed. Spirit is all, and it annuls the cold. All is Spirit and you are whole—all well.

### Catarrh.

You know that God is everywhere. God is Spirit and is with you; is all around you. The sweet healing Spirit that is health itself is all about you. You breathe it with every breath. It is all through you, over you, and you are one with it. Nothing can come near you to hurt you for it protects you. You must be perfectly well in this presence and you are well and whole—clean and wholesome, now.

### Catarrh.

You cannot have any trouble in your head for you are always in the presence of God, and God is perfect health. You live and move and breathe in God, thus you also are perfect health and nothing else can come near you. There is nothing else in all the universe, for God fills all space. You are perfectly whole; filled with the Holy Ghost.

### Weakness With Fear.

You have no fear; you are not afraid of anything. There is nothing to fear for God is your protection. He is as near You are to yourself, and no harm can come near you. God is health itself and strength itself and nothing else can enter His presence. His health is your health and His strength is your strength. You are perfectly well and strong, now.

### Debility.

You are in the presence of God always. God is life; vitality. You are one with God for He made you of His own substance. Thus you are one with this Spirit that is vitality all around you, in you, through you. You breathe in every instant. You are one with Spirit and there is no separation. *You* are Spirit, you must be, for there is nothing else for you to be. You overflow with vitality; you are happy, joyous and buoyant; all life and vitality. You are happiness, strength, and love. You want to laugh and sing to express this vitality. You are all life. You are whole and perfect because one with God.

### Nervousness.

You are surrounded by the Spirit of Peace. It envelops you as the atmosphere does. You are one with It. You breathe It with every breath and It fills you with peace and rest. Nothing can come near to disturb your or make you afraid of anything. There is no nervousness in this presence. Spirit is health and strength and fills you with health and strength. You are strong and calm and perfectly well.

## Or This.

God is with you. God is peace and comfort. Be still and let peace steal through you till you feel the very strength of God; till you feel strong to stand firm against the world, needing no help, no one to lean upon. You are sufficient for yourself, because you are one with the Spirit that is God. There is nothing about you that is not strong and well, just as you have chosen it to be. You are satisfied. You are full of courage and sweet peace.

## Or This.

The sweet Spirit of comfort is all around you. (Several times.) It is through you and in you. You are bathed in Spirit. You are Spirit. You are whole and comforted and satisfied.

## Brain Exhaustion.

God holds you in his arms. He bears you up. You need not even think for yourself. He cares for you, He rests you. He has nothing for you but peace, comfort and strength. Rest in the Lord for your health is established.

## Or This.

All is God—all is God—all is God. You are rested and refreshed. The Spirit that is God enfolds you, surrounds you, and rests you. You rest in God you are in God and there is no separation. You are one with Him. You rest in God.

### Or This.

There is nothing in all the universe but Spirit. You are Spirit and breathe this Spirit. It is perfect health, strength, peace, and there is nothing else anywhere. You were created of health, strength and peace. You are perfect health, perfect Strength, perfect peace, and you show forth nothing else. You are whole.

### Bright's Disease, Or Kindred Troubles.

You are in the presence of God. In this presence there can be nothing unlike itself. Spirit is a fire that consumes all that is not perfect. You are cleansed, purified. The Spirit of health and strength is all about you, you breathe it, you are one with it. You stand forth whole and perfect, one with God.

### Anything Acute with Great Pain.

You are in the presence of God; that presence is peace, rest, strength, and it fills you with peace, rest and strength. You rest in this presence with perfect content. It is health and safety. Pain cannot enter this presence. You are free from any pain. You are whole and perfect;

### Or This.

God is everywhere, you are in His presence. He is perfect health so there is nothing about you but perfect health. There is no pain. You breathe health, you are in it, you are one with it. You *are* perfect health. You are whole like God who made you, for you are one with Him. You are whole like God who made you, for you are one with Him. He made you from himself, like himself, thus you are perfect in peace.

### Epilepsy Or Anything Having Fear.

You are not afraid of anything, for you are safe. God folds you round with loving care and protection. You know that God is everywhere. You have heard that if you go down into the sea, or even under the earth, that God is there. You cannot get away from God.

You know that God cannot be sick, sickness cannot enter His presence. You are always in His presence, and each breath you draw is from God just as you breathe the air. You cannot be sick for you breathe only health. You are well for God enfolds you. His everlasting arms uphold you. You are whole.

### Or This.

There is nothing to fear. You are safe. The sweet Spirit is all around you. It enfolds you every moment and you feel It. You can lean upon God as upon your mother. His arms are about you and you can rest in His care and power. He is intelligence and you are intelligence. You are quick and bright. Your memory is perfect. You are strong and whole, for God gives you perfect strength and health every instant.

### Tumor Or Swelling.

You refuse to have any thought that can make a tumor. When the thought is gone the tumor is gone also. Spirit cannot enlarge or swell, and you are Spirit. Spirit knows no such thoughts. You have no tumor, for you are pure and clean and whole. You are Spirit and perfect. You are free. You are whole, now.

### Heart Disease.

There is nothing to fear for you are surrounded entirely by Spirit—God. You breathe Spirit and you need not even try to breathe for yourself. Spirit will breathe for you and fill you with strength and vigor and peace. It breathes for you so gently that all you need is just to wait, be still, and let it breathe through you. You are full of courage and hope and strength. There is nothing else in Spirit. You have nothing to do. Spirit is all and does all. You are Spirit and whole and perfect. Peace is Is your life and your rest.

### Or This.

There is no fear, for God is with you. Lean on Him. He is your support and breathes for you; takes care of you. You are resting in the right. You are strong for you have strength from God every instant. This sweet, breathing Spirit is all around you. It is in you. Through you breathes for you; lives for you. It quickens you and fills you with vitality. You are alive with It. You are one with It. You live and move and have your being in Spirit. You are strong and sound and whole in the Peace of God.

### Or This.

This beautiful, gentle, kind, Father—Spirit, sustains, upholds, steadies you. You can lean upon It as upon a mother.

It is mother as well as father, tender, loving, soothing, ministering to every need. Peace is close to you. You are one with it, made of it, and from it. It is the only life you have. You breathe it and you need not even try to breathe for yourself, as it breathes for you and through you, filling you with strength and health, and life and vitality.

### Blindness.

"Let there be light." You are bathed in a sea of light for God is light and He is all around you. You are in the glorious presence of God always. God is sight itself. You see with His sight. He sees through you and for you. You have perfect sight now. "All is light."

### Or This.

"God saw the light and it was good." You are in the presence of God always and you see the light that it is good. There is nothing but light for God is light. God is everywhere and He is all. All is light—all is sight. You have perfect sight for God sees in you and through you and for you. All is light for all is God. You cannot imagine any darkness where God is and God is wherever you are. Thus you are enveloped in light. You see perfectly.

### Fear Of Any Person Or Influence.

You know that you are one with God, thus you know that all power is yours. You have dominion over all flesh and fleshly ways. Speak the word of power and it shall be done. Power is all, there is no fear, and there cannot be. You are absolutely free. You are power; assert it. You are one with God. Lean upon Him and He will protect you. God is your defense and protection. God folds you round with safety and protection. You are safe. You have dominion over all the earth. Use it.

### Weakness, Called "Run Down."

You are strong, you are strong, you are perfect strength. You cannot think of weakness being near God or where He is. He is where you are all the time. Thus you are, and you must be strong in His strength. There is nothing but strength in all the universe; it is full of strength. You breathe it each instant.

You are strength through and through, and show forth nothing else. You know you are strong. You get your strength from God and He has plenty for you. You are strong and vigorous and can do all you want to do. You have endurance unlimited. All is strength and all is yours for all is God. You are one with God.

### Treatments Through Realizing God's Presence.

In treating people, in the room with them, we say first, "I am one with God," until we feel so at one with Him, feel it so strongly, that we know that no mortal condition or thought can be in our presence. We know that our presence annihilates and cannot admit sickness, disease or trouble, or rather that they *are* not. The patient being in the presence of God, our realization of it is surely sufficient to cure whatever he believes in. The cure is in our strong feeling. The presence of God destroys any idea of sickness as an alkali eats up the acid. It is not there, it has vanished as dew before the sun. We feel this so strongly that no words are needed. Our feeling is like a song without words that penetrates every fiber of the patient's being with harmony, which is health. We see only health, and say it is finished.

When we feel in this way we cannot say, "you are being healed," or anything about healing, for it does not seem true to us. Our idea is of everything, completed, already done, as it always was, and is, and shall be forever. There is nothing going on at all, nothing to be done. All was done once for all in the beginning and forever.

It seems as if some patients could grasp a few words better than a long argument, so we tell such a great deal about God and very little about themselves, except that they are one with God. We do not speak of the mortal, as that is recognizing it, and we cannot even deny what we did not recognize. If we say a thing is not true we own the possibility of its being thought true.

When we treat absently we can bring the patient to us in thought, like this:

Here we are in this blessed presence, and here is peace and health and happiness. This presence is love. And love is strength. It is around us and in us and through us. It *is* us, and we are It. No burdens, pains or sickness can be here at all. In this fountain is whatever we want. We are bathed in the sea of Spirit; the infinite sea of love. We breathe the sweet spirit of peace; we are full of it; we breathe the sweet spirit of peace; we are full of it; we bathe in it and are whole. All is health, strength, peace, love, comfort and courage. These fill you. You are health and peace. You are whole.

Or this: There is only God here. There is only God here. Let all the earth keep silence before Him. (Earth meaning flesh.) There can be no pain, nothing mortal here. God is here, the mortal is not, for both cannot be in one place. You are whole and sound.—If one way of treating does not cure we must try another, for different people require different methods in thought just as much as in medicine. The idiosyncrasy is of mind not body.

For a tired person, or weak: I am one with God, thus I am one with peace. All is peace and rest in my presence. Peace is falling all around you. We are filled with peace. Peace comes down from the ceiling, up from the floor, our from the walls. We breathe it, you rest in it. All is peace and rest. There is nothing else. Peace—peace—peace—strength—strength—rest. When we say this we feel the peace falling down about the patient and see her quiet and content.

## For Good Judgment.

There is only Spirit. It fills the universe so that there is no place for you outside of it. You are in it. You are one with it. You are it. There is no room for anything but Justice, Wisdom, Power and Peace, in the universe actually filled with God. You are so truly one with God that you are Wisdom, Power, Justice, and all your decisions are wise and just. Your judgment is sound and perfect. You know exactly what to do always.

## For Rheumatism, Neuralgia, Or Any Pain.

You have no pain at all, for you are Spirit and Spirit knows no pain at all. Spirit cannot know sickness or pain. You *are* Spirit and cannot have them. You are free from them for you are filled with Spirit. You are Spirit. Spirit is all around you. You live in it, are one with it. There is nothing but Spirit. You are sound and whole. The hush and calm of God fall down through you and you rest.

## Self-Treatments.

We must praise the Spirit a great deal; not because it needs our praise, but because praise is the law of love. We must thank Spirit for all the blessings we desire, as that is praying as if we had already received, which we were told by Jesus is the true prayer.

## Self-Treatment Against Sickness.

Most Holy Spirit, I thank Thee that Thou hast given me the blessing I have asked for. It is mine. Sweet Spirit is health I praise Thee that Thou dost pour over me perfect health; that Thou art infinite health; that I am made of Thy substance; am one with Thee; am in Thee; am Spirit like Thee, with Thee, and in Thee. I bless Thee that I also am perfect health; that I am whole; that I cannot know sickness, disease, or pain of any kind. I breathe nothing but health for there is nothing else. Thou art all Spirit and Thou art health. I in Thee and Thou in me forevermore. I think Thee that I am whole now.

## For Health.

Sweet, blessed Spirit, thou art all around me like the bright sunshine. I am bathed in Spirit as in the sun bath of summer. And as the sun is life and health vigor, so Spirit is life itself, health itself, and vigor itself. I am Spirit and one with this Spirit that enfolds me. As the sun drives away fog and clouds, so Spirit drives away all error that gives cloudy thoughts which show out as sickness and disease. As the sun always shines, no matter how many clouds keep us from seeing it, so Spirit is always here, health is always here, we cannot get away from sunshine unless we hide away in the dark; it is everywhere and warms and revives everything, neither do we get away from Thee, O Divine Spirit.

Thou art always here even when our sick thoughts keep us from knowing Thee. Health and vigor everlasting are always here. I praise Thee, O Spirit, that I am one with health and vigor; that I am health itself and can show forth only health.

## Against Weakness.

Sweet healing Spirit, I praise Thee that Thou dost surround me with strength and health. When I breathe, I breathe Thee, O Spirit! So I breathe only strength. I am Spirit like Thee, thus I cannot know weakness at all. Spirit cannot be weak, cannot know any weakness. There is no weakness; it is but resting, waiting till strength fills me. I thank Thee, O Spirit! For the strength and vitality that I feel in every part of my being. I am one with Thee, made of thy substance. I am breathing Thee. I am breathing Thee. I breathe only strength. I am one with all strength; it is around me and in me. I am strength for I am one with Thee, O blessed spirit! I am whole.

## Against Pain.

I thank thee, O Father-Spirit, that I am Spirit and am free from any knowledge of pain. I am Spirit and Spirit is free as the air. I am free and cannot know, or have pain at all. What I call pain is but some wrong thought leaving me. I refuse to have any thoughts that make pictures of pain on the body. They cannot enter my mind any more for I am filled with Spirit. I am Spirit and know nothing but peace and comfort. Spirit eases and soothes me through and through. I know only ease and comfort and peace. Spirit is all, and I am only Spirit—Spirit—Spirit. I am whole and perfect now.

## For Peace.

Blessed Spirit, I thank Thee that Thou dost envelop me with Thy sweet peace. It fills me; it covers me like a mantle; it broods over me with the tenderness of mother. It comes down from above, and up from below, and comes to me from all about. It is through me and in me. I am indeed It. Thou leadest me, gracious Spirit, and my ways are pleasantness, my path all peace. Wherever I go Thou art leading me. I praise Thee that I am one with peace; one with Thee. I praise Thee that I am Thine own creation. Thy presence is always with me; in it is perfect rest. All is peace; there is nothing else, for Thou art all.

### Against Fear.

I can fear no evil for Thou art with me, O blessed Spirit! There is only God in all universe. I am in the presence of God always, everywhere, and cannot get away from It. I thank Thee that Thou art infinite courage. God make me in His own image, thus I am full of courage and fearlessness and boldness. I am one with God from whom I came forth; in whom I live and move. I am of His substance—Spirit. Thus, I am courage itself, boldness itself. I thank Thee, O Spirit! That Thou art all about me, and nothing can come near me; that I am safe from all evil in Thee, as Spirit knows no evil.

### Against Opposition.

I thank Thee, O God! That in Thee all is safety and peace. There can be no opposition in Spirit, therefore against me there is no opposition. I am Spirit and one with Thee. I praise Thee that Thou art all; that I can lean on Thee, finding safety and protection.

### Against Poverty.

Great and bountiful Spirit, I rejoice in the full supply that Thou hast given me. I thank Thee that I am supplied with all that I can ask for. Thou art all good. The symbol of good is gold, thus a plentiful supply of gold is mine, for Thou art the fullness of supply. It is thy delight to give; Thou art more willing to give, than we are to receive. I am supplied with all I want, for I am one with Thee. All that is Thine is mine. All power is given unto me, in Thee, therefore all things whatsoever I ask for are mine. I thank Thee, I bless Thee, I praise Thee, for all thy riches that are heaped upon me. The Almighty in my defense and I have plenty of silver.

## Against Trouble.

O blessed Spirit! Thou dost take care of me and protect me from all that seems like trouble. I thank Thee that thou art a dear friend upon whom I can lean; upon whom I can rest and be comforted and strengthened. I can lean my head against Thee and be rested. I can fly to Thee for protection from all assaults of trouble or circumstance, and Thou wilt cover me as the hen covers her little ones. Thou dost brood over us with loving tenderness and care, and protection. I trust in Thee. Thou dost guide and lead me. I am safe and happy for Thou art all, and I am in thee forever.

## Against Injustice.

I thank Thee, O God, that no one can be unjust to me; That there is no such thing as injustice. What is called injustice falls away from me like arrows from an armor, for I am encompassed by Thy angels. I am protected for I am one with God and God is perfect justice. There is no injustice possible in a universe filled with the God who is justice. Thou art all. Then justice is all. As I am in Thee I am in justice. I am one with complete justice, and nothing can come near to disturb me, not even in the least. "The angel of the Lord encampeth round about" all the children of God, so I am free from all thought of injustice.

## Against Malice.

I thank Thee and bless Thee, O gentle Spirit! That in Thy realm, malicious thoughts are unknown. I cannot fear them for they cannot enter the sphere where I dwell with Thee. I am above such things. They are only like a distant fog that cannot come nearer. The bright sunshine of Thy presence prevents anything like malice from reaching me. I am safe in Thee and fear not for a moment though ten thousand mortal minds were directed to me with malice intent. I am Spirit and Spirit is free—entirely free—from all that is mortal. Thou art my defense and my shield. I am content.

## For Efficiency.

Blessed Spirit! I praise Thee that Thou hast created me efficient; that I am surrounded by efficiency; that I can do whatever there is for me to do, as God works through me to will and to do. I bless Thee that I know that I am one with Thee and there is no separation possible. Thus I am one with efficiency itself, and am capable and efficient and can do all things, God working through me.

## For Judgment.

God is all there is and God is Spirit. There is only Spirit and it fills me so that there is no separation. We are One. Spirit is perfect Judgment, thus I am one with perfect judgment and know just what to do under all circumstances. I thank Thee, O, Father! That Thy judgment is mine; that Thy counsel is mine; that I am wise and capable of judging correctly upon all matters and occasions. I am one with Thee, therefore perfect in all ways. My judgment is sound and perfect always.

## For Power.

True wisdom is knowledge; knowledge is power; power is God. I am one with God so I am one with all power. All power is given unto me for I and my Father are one. All things are mine through God who giveth me power. I am master over all things. I have dominion over all the earth. Because my word is the word of God. I can by my word banish sickness, trouble and poverty; they cannot come anywhere near me or near anyone around me. I know what to do always; my decisions are just and perfect. I am so at one with God that I am power expressed, wisdom expressed, and judgment manifest. I am power and can do all things. When I say I am power I feel strong and masterful, yet humble and gentle. I reign over the earth and earthly ways and thoughts. In Spirit there is only God, and God reigns. I thank Thee, O Father! That I have all things that I could desire. All is mine for I am Thine.

## Against Intemperance In Anything.

I am all Spirit and cannot be intemperate in any way. Spirit cannot think wrong thoughts; cannot have immoderate desires or foolish wishes; cannot covet or long for what is not its own. Spirit cannot see rum or tobacco; does not know them; cannot touch them. Spirit knows none of these things. It is free from the thought of them. They cannot affect spirit. I am Spirit and cannot be moved by them. I am perfectly temperate in all ways and all things. I thank Thee, O Spirit! That I am Spirit and cannot know any intemperance; cannot see or touch liquor or tobacco at all. To me they are nothing—nothing.

We use thought much as we would medicine, for it is the only true medicine. It stimulants are required, stimulating thoughts or words are used; if quieting, soporific remedies are needed, soothing thoughts are used, and so on for all conditions. As an instance, let us give a case we recently heard of:

A healer was called to a "dying" man. The doctors had pronounced his doom and friends were waiting to see the consummation of it. After asking all to leave the room, that there might be no counteracting influence, the healer sat by the man and said (mentally), "All is Life—all is Life—all is God—all is God—God is Life—God is Life—you are one with God—you are Life—Life—Life—Life"—repeating all these words in a quick, energetic manner till the room, bed and man were all charged with life. The patient felt it and revived, breathed more easily and became warm; the color came into his face. Then he was restless and said his head ached. The healer then spoke soothing words, saying, "There, there, lie still and slumber," over and over till the patient was asleep and rested as calmly as a child.

This healer was not afraid of doctors or medicine. The power of God, or that *is* God, is more than all medicines, and can be demonstrated so to be. We should never stop to quibble over insignificant matters; and all that is material is insignificant. We must call forth life whenever we can. It is the duty of every one to continue in the body and show forth true life, and we must help to bring that to pass as much as possible.

To be a scientist is not to lose our common sense; on the contrary it should be to have more than ever before. In studying science we should never think that neglect of personal appearance is a mark of being spiritual, or of being occupied with spiritual things. We must never neglect person or house. The without is as the within. Those who are scrupulously clean without are most apt to be pure and clean within. "Cleanliness is next to Godliness."

The Free Masons are good examples to the world in one respect—they protect their own brethren; never speaking ill of them or to them. Should not Scientists, who claim to follow in the footsteps of Jesus Christ, do as well? Does not the law teach that if we deal unkindly or unjustly with one who is one with God, that the unkindness or harshness will glance off from that one back to ourselves and work the harm to us instead? Did we never hear these words of the law—"Whoso shall offend one of these little ones, it were better for him that a milestone were hanged about his neck, and he were drowned in the depth of the sea." 'Woe to that man by who, the offense cometh."

## THE END.

NOTES

# NOTES

## EMMA C. HOPKINS BOOKS PUBLISHED BY:

ECH Theological Association, Inc.

S.T.T.'S
Spiritual Law in The Natural World
www.highwatch.net

Bible Interpretation Series 1-9
The Gospel Series
Judgment Series in Spiritual Science
Radiant I Am and Self Treatment
High Mysticism
Resume
Drops of Gold
Class Lessons 1888
Esoteric Philosophy: Deeper Teachings in Spiritual Science
www.wisewomanpress.com

CPSIA information can be obtained at www.ICGtesting.com
Printed in the USA
LVOW120928281112

309126LV00003B/374/P